Indo-Caribbean Indenture

Indo-Caribbean Indenture
Resistance and Accommodation, 1838–1920

Lomarsh Roopnarine

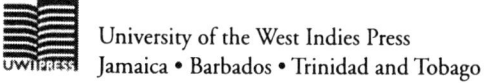
University of the West Indies Press
Jamaica • Barbados • Trinidad and Tobago

University of the West Indies Press
7A Gibraltar Hall Road   Mona
Kingston 7   Jamaica
www.uwipress.com

© 2007 by Lomarsh Roopnarine
All rights reserved. Published 2007

11 10 09 08 07   5 4 3 2 1

Roopnarine, Lomarsh.
Indo-Caribbean indenture: resistance and accommodation, 1838–1920 / Lomarsh Roopnarine.

p. cm.

Includes bibliographical references.

ISBN: 978-976-640-185-6

1. Indentured servants – West Indies, British – History – 19th century. 2. Alien labour, East Indian – West Indies, British – History – 19th century. 3. Sugar workers – West Indies, British – History – 19th century. 4. Contract labour – West Indies, British – History – 19th century. 5. West Indies, British – Emigration and immigration – History – 19th century. I. Title.

F2191.E27R66 2007   927.9'004914

Book and cover design by Robert Kwak.

Set in Univers and Garamond.

Printed in Canada.

Indo-Caribbean Indenture: Resistance and Accommodation, 1838–1920 is dedicated to my father, Roopnarine Lachhman (also called Fred Lalla), who died suddenly of a heart attack in June 2004 in Syracuse, New York, precisely at the time I was doing the revisions for this book. He was almost seventy-seven years old. For over four decades, my father worked on Plantation Skeldon (formerly called Eliza and Mary) along the banks of the Corentyne River in Guyana, first as a Creole gang member, then as a cane cutter, and finally as a shovel man. He was a pensioner. Much of the information in this book relates to his grandparents', his parents', and finally his experience as an East Indian in the Caribbean. Unfortunately, he did not live long enough to see (he could not read) one of his own children write about his family's indentured experience and the larger Caribbean East Indian community. May God bless his soul and those of others who laboured and died on those harsh tropical sugar plantations.

Contents

Acknowledgements	ix
Introduction	3
Chapter 1 Migration and Recruitment	13
Chapter 2 Domination and Modes of Resistance	36
Chapter 3 Cultural Change and Continuity: Caste and the Joint Family System	62
Chapter 4 Indo-Caribbean Women: Daughters of Sacrifice and Survival	87
Conclusion	108
Appendices	121
Notes	136
Bibliography	154
Index	168

Acknowledgements

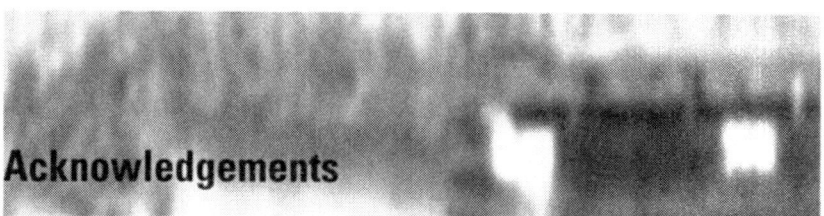

Indo-Caribbean Indenture: Resistance and Accommodation, 1838–1920 is a result of the efforts of many individuals and institutions. I benefited greatly from my interaction with my dissertation director, Dr Colbert Nepaulsingh, at the State University of New York at Albany. Thanks to Dr Liliana Goldin and Dr Edna Acosta-Belen. My gratitude to Dr Verene Shepherd of the University of the West Indies at Mona for her comments on a revised version of the manuscript. Thanks also to the two anonymous reviewers for their comments and criticisms. Special thanks to my wife, Dr Jennifer Roopnarine, for all her help.

"A non-violent fight is like the edge of a sword, sharpened on the whetstone of the heart."

– Mohandas Karamchand Gandhi

"With Truth in one hand and Labour in the other, Labour would be invincible, . . . for Labour is the only power in the World."

– Mohandas Karamchand Gandhi

Introduction

The Literature on Caribbean East Indians

Over the past forty years and, in particular, since the first conference in Trinidad in 1975 on the theme, there has been growing interest in the study of Caribbean East Indians. While there has been some duplication of information, there has also been some outstanding scholarship in history and indenture, culture, politics, gender, education, ethnicity, religion, caste, migration, literature, music, sports, and identity.[1] Despite these studies, several aspects of Indo-Caribbean indenture deserve more attention. For example, Verene Shepherd has established that the study of Caribbean East Indians has predominantly focused on the larger territories – Guyana, Trinidad and Suriname – where East Indians are the majority population.[2] Less attention has been paid to areas in the Caribbean where East Indians are a minority. More attention has been paid to the English-speaking Caribbean than to the French, Dutch and Danish Caribbean.

The majority of studies on East Indians, particularly those focusing on the indenture period, have treated indentured servitude in the Caribbean as a neo-slave system. These studies tell an impressive story of indentured servitude: its fraudulent recruitment practices, rigorous discipline, authoritarian management, the development of settled communities and the abolition of indentured emigration. Hugh Tinker correctly concluded that East Indians were moved from a society in India, however degrading that society might have been, to an exploitative one, where their values were considered secondary to the production of sugar.[3] Brinsley Samaroo writes that a substantial number of indentured servants were not successful in establishing themselves in the Caribbean, and so they had little to lose by returning to India.[4] Certainly one cannot understate or underestimate the role of the colonial regime in executing and maintaining the exploitative nature of the plantation system. Strategies of hierarchization and marginalization were employed in the management of colonial societies. Colonies, by the very nature of their subordinate status, were not involved in the decision-making process. The imperial system acted or operated according to general and broad principles rather than to individual cases. Thus, within the imperial system, there was also internal colonialism in which the dominant groups exploited the less fortunate in highly organized and regimented ways. At a minimum level, Caribbean society was based on the organization of the production of tropical staples for imperial and international markets. Everything else was secondary to this aim. The end result was that Old World cultures were subdued, while at the same time new codes of conformity and expectations were introduced. The negative effects of this preoccupation are ubiquitously documented, and in the case of the indenture system, the two most striking documentations are from two indentured servants: song writer Labehari Sharma[5] and Bechu, a critic of the indenture system.[6]

But is there another side to the indenture system? Why did indentured servants continue to come to the Caribbean in spite of the authoritarian structure of the plantation system? Not all emigrants were deceived into leaving their homeland. While in the Caribbean, did they merely accept that the plantation system was too powerful to resist, resigning themselves to what was expected of them: to provide plantation labour in a docile manner? Did they resist openly only when pushed beyond limits? V.S. Naipaul stated that one would be surprised at what East Indians have achieved in the Caribbean considering they arrived empty-handed. Of course, East Indians did not really arrive in the Caribbean totally empty-handed. They brought some cultural items such as pots, pans, *lota* and blankets. One cannot, however, ignore the fact that neither their non-material culture – beliefs, values and acumen – nor their ways of doing things – common pattern of behaviours – were lost in the migration process. They certainly brought memories of their culture and traditions. Even begging, a socially acceptable practice in India, was brought to the Caribbean. East Indians soon found out, however, that their cultural beliefs were at odds with the predominantly Eurocentric and Afrocentric Caribbean. Subsequently, some of these values were simply suppressed. Yet the well-known mantra in the United States that you can take an individual out of the community, but you cannot take the community out of the individual can also apply to East Indian indentured servants. The colonial regime took East Indians out of India, but they never took India out of the East Indians. This is not to say that East Indian culture was a monolithic entity with firm boundaries where it was conceived to be stuck in time and space without any prospect of historical change. East Indians, like the Europeans and Africans before them, deliberately tried to re-create miniatures of their homeland in the Caribbean.

Within this symbiotic relationship – India and the Caribbean – East Indians in the settler communities fabricated, formed and shaped their identities, as well as their economic future, individually and collectively. This study examines how indentured servants individually and collectively used indentured emigration to better their lives, resist domination, reproduce and reinvent their culture, adapt and turn adverse circumstances to their advantage. This was possible because indentured servants understood the pros and cons of the plantation system and manipulated it with minimum disadvantage to themselves under everyday forms of resistance in the Caribbean and India. These forms of resistance were not always obvious. Moreover, the adjustment and adaptation of indentured servants to Caribbean society were not necessarily a result of pressure from the dominant class but rather were influenced by their own actions, activities and attitudes, amid some degree of conformity. We are yet to have a balanced view of the East Indian Caribbean indenture experience. We know little about the adaptive and adaxial capacity of the indentured servants, and more about the negative experience of the indenture system. It is not so much what East Indians have achieved – other ethnic groups have also done remarkably well – but rather how they were able to do so. To begin to address or even to understand this process, we have to revisit the indenture period.

An Overview of Indenture Service

Indentured service occurred in two phases: from the seventeenth to the eighteenth centuries and from the mid-nineteenth to the early twentieth centuries. In the first phase, about three hundred thousand western Europeans – English, French, Germans, Irish, Scots – were brought to North America and the Caribbean.[7] In the second phase, about two and one-half million non-Europeans – mostly East Indians and Chinese, but also substantial numbers of Africans, Javanese, Japanese and Pacific Islanders – were brought to the Caribbean, East Africa, Fiji, Hawaii, Latin America, Mauritius, Natal, Sri Lanka, Strait Settlements and Queensland. Except for Fiji, Hawaii, Natal and Queensland, where there was no experience of plantation slavery, both phases were deeply affected by the presence of slavery, but in opposite ways.[8] Whereas the indentured service of the first phase was supplanted by slavery, the indentured service of the second phase followed the abolition of slavery.[9] East Indian indentured servants began to arrive in the Caribbean in the second phase of the indentured service because of the gradual withdrawal of Africans from plantation labour following emancipation in the British (1838), Danish (1848), French (1848) and Dutch Caribbean (1863), and the failure of various immigration schemes from Africa, China, Europe, Java, Madeira, Portugal and within the Caribbean.

Table 1: Number of Indentured East Indian Emigrants Introduced to the Caribbean, 1838–1920

British Guiana	238,960	Grenada	3,200
Trinidad	143,939	Belize	3,000
Dutch Guiana	43,404	St Vincent	2,472
Guadeloupe	42,236	St Lucia	2,300
Jamaica	37,027	St Kitts	361
Martinique	25,404	Nevis	342
French Guiana	8,500	Danish St Croix	325

More East Indians would have been brought to the New World, especially to Cuba and St Croix, had not the British government turned down the Spanish and Danish governments' request for indentured labourers because of evidence of East Indian emigrants being abused abroad. The Spanish government then brought Chinese contract labourers instead of Indians to Cuba, while the Danish government used mainly black contract labourers from the Eastern Caribbean (down islanders) in St Croix.[10] The indenture system brought about five hundred thousand East Indians (*Girmitiyas*) to work the plantations in the Caribbean (*Karma Bhumi*/land of work). Of this total, about a quarter returned home (*Janma Bhumi*/land of birth), while the remainder stayed and accepted the Caribbean as their new-found home; and by the 1920s, East Indians had come to form the majority population in Guyana (43.5 per cent), Trinidad (33 per cent) and Suriname (37 per cent). Table 2 shows the number of East Indian emigrants who were entitled to and accepted return passages from Jamaica, British Guiana and Trinidad to India from 1850 to 1864.

Table 2: Number of East Indians Who Returned to India, 1850–1864

Colony	Years	Numbers
British Guiana	1850–1864	4,984
Jamaica	1850–1858	1,722
Trinidad	1851–1861	2,680

Source: House of Commons, *Parliamentary Papers*, vol.18 (3526), *The Twenty-fifth General Report of the Colonial Land and Emigration Commissioners* (London: HMSO, 1865), 90 (appendix).

The East Indian indentured service was a labour contract system that bound men, women, children and even families for a stipulated number of years on the Caribbean sugar plantations. The indentured servants were required to work on a plantation for five years on a fixed daily wage (about one shilling a day). At the end of the five years, they had the option to re-indenture for another five years and qualified for industrial residence in the colonies as well as an entitlement to free repatriation. Some indentured servants contributed to or paid their own passage back to India. The indenture system was governed by a series of elaborate labour ordinances often defined in written terms, which essentially gave the planters the right to exploit the labour of these servants until their contracts were over. Any breaches of contract, refusal to work, unsatisfactory work or absence from work were punishable crimes that resulted in imprisonment for the labourer. The indentured servants had some rights but very often these rights were abused. Despite these impediments, many continued to come to the Caribbean in light of adverse and destitute conditions in India and the prospect of a better life abroad. The indenture system offered those who were poor opportunities to improve their lot through migration.

Their presence on the plantations helped, if not revolutionized, the sugar industries, which otherwise would have collapsed:

> Within the sugar cane industry, the overall productivity of indentured labour remained below that of slavery. But, between 1870 and 1880, the proportion of the world's sugar cane it produced increased from 23 per cent to 29 per cent. In doing so, it partially compensated for a decline of slave production from 52 per cent to 37 per cent, helping to ensure that, even in the early 1880s, at least 66 per cent of the world's sugar cane remained the product of bonded labour.[11]

Apart from indentured service providing the opportunity for migration and the release from afflictive and adverse conditions in India, the system was beneficial in some ways, especially after indentured servants had served out their terms of contract. They were rewarded with land and grant money to set up businesses. These incentives encouraged indentured East Indians to stay in the Caribbean. Their inclination to stay was particularly welcomed by the planters, because it was seen as a solution to the labour problem. The colonial government drafted rules and regulations concerning recruitment, transportation, working and living conditions on the plantations to safeguard and protect indentured workers. But these mechanisms were not effectively employed, and soon the indenture system was criticized for replicating the evils of the middle passage and slavery. The British government in India refrained from taking an active part in condoning or condemning the indenture system. Its position was not to get mixed up in the transactions and bargains between the Caribbean and India until the rise of the Indian nationalist movement in the early twentieth century.[12] Mounting pressure from the Indian National Congress, renewed agitation in India and the Caribbean, and the recommendation of the Commission of Enquiry on conditions of East Indians abroad in the early twentieth century forced the British imperial government in India to reconsider its position. In 1920, under war conditions, the imperialist government abolished East Indian indentured emigration and effectively stopped the flood of indentures to the Caribbean. It was the first time in three centuries that all forms of labour became legally free in the Americas.[13]

The Sources

Data from primary sources were gathered at the Colonial Record Office in London, the India Record Office in the British Library in London, Guyana National Archives in Georgetown, from British Parliamentary Papers at the New York State Library and at the University of Albany, State University of New York, Whim Library in St Croix and the Baa Library in St. Thomas. The secondary sources consist of scholarly texts, reports, depositions, journals, and were collected from various universities in the United States and the Caribbean. Additionally, ethnographic sources were gathered from visits to East Indian communities in the Caribbean. Creative literature has been used to examine Indo-Caribbean family relations: caste, marriage, joint family and gender. Literary works are important to this study, because they often express feelings, ideas and experiences not easily accessible in historical accounts.

The oral sources consist of interviews with scores of East Indians between 1996 and 2004 in Guyana, Suriname, Trinidad, St Croix, St Lucia, St Vincent, New York City and Jersey City. These subjects, aged twenty to eighty-five, had knowledge of indentured service through family and oral traditions. The younger subjects interviewed had an intense interest in East Indian Caribbean culture and thus provided information based on what they had learned as children. The older subjects knew how their parents and grandparents worked on the sugar plantations under indenture. Some of the older subjects could read, speak or write only Hindi, Pidgin English and some English. All subjects had lived near, or had some affiliation with, the sugar plantations.

The interview asked for biographical information and what the subjects knew or remembered about the indenture system. It was conducted in a face-to-face question-and-answer format or by telephone. However, most of the sources for this study were gathered from written original and secondary sources. Since indentured service was abolished about eighty years ago, and therefore it was not possible to speak with indentured servants, their voices or agencies from various narratives, work and folk songs were examined. Narratives, work and folk songs, folklore and storytelling of indentured servants were important to this study because they satisfied the shortcomings of historical records and the claim of some informants that they had no knowledge of the indenture system. These materials not only coincided with what some the informants said about the indenture system, but they contained information on resistance, cultural continuity and change, and gender relations, themes central to this study. Moreover, these materials revealed a surprising degree of literacy among indentured servants and provocative discussions based especially on wage claims and sexual abuse.

The Focus of the Study

Chapter 1 begins with the argument that the arrival of East Indians in the Caribbean corresponded with the labour scarcity caused by the gradual withdrawal of freed Africans from plantation labour and the expansion of world capitalism. Attempts will be made to move away from the overused, worn-out push/pull model to explain indentured emigration, although one cannot totally deny that beneath any migration theory there are some elements of this model. Nineteenth-century East Indian emigration was related to the expansion of western imperialism and colonialism.[14] Certainly, some internal factors, such as social and caste oppression, caused East Indians to emigrate,[15] but internal factors were exacerbated and expostulated by the superstructure of the more powerful capitalist development.

Chapter 2 shows how indentured servants resisted and manipulated the indenture system. It argues that despite the fact that indentured service was an institution set up for appropriating labour, goods and services to fulfil the demands of the dominant plantocracy class, indentured servants had a meaningful social existence outside the immediate domain of the dominant. They were not totally subdued by the hegemonic plantation system.

While no one denies that indentured servants suffered under an unjust plantation system, they were also, as a subordinate class, capable of penetrating and manipulating that system. They lashed out against the indenture system in various forms: feigned sickness, strikes, riots and so on (overt actions). Behind the backs of the planter class, indentured servants created a social space in which they were able to improve their lives (covert actions). East Indians understood the "hidden transcript" of the dominant class, and they manipulated it to their minimum disadvantage[16] (like the dominant class, indentured servants themselves had also a "hidden transcript" at their disposal), without risking open defiant confrontation with the plantocracy,[17] although violent clashes between East Indians and the dominant class did occur on the plantations. Since indentured servants were never really interested in overturning the plantocracy, guerilla-style, comparison and analysis of the "hidden transcripts" of both the dominant and subordinate classes is an instructive way of understanding East Indian resistance under indenture.

Chapter 3 begins with how indentured servants maintained certain important cultural mores, while at the same time willingly dispensing with others. East Indians fought to retain certain integral cultural characteristics, but others became diluted and diced in light of confrontation with the more powerful plantation system. Nonetheless, through the process of cultural continuity and change, indentured servants were better off in the Caribbean than they were in India. Cultural continuity guided East Indians to resist and to deal with the plantation system. Cultural change, whether imposed or voluntary, inadvertently served to get rid of wanton aspects of the servile East Indian caste system, which relegated the lower castes, in particular, to the bottom of the traditional economic, social and cultural spheres in India. Indentured servants were able to dispense with certain oppressive customs without adopting or forcing themselves into new chains of bondage in the Caribbean.

Chapter 4 examines the position of East Indian women under indenture and shows how they used the system to improve their lives. It analyses the position of Indian women in India with regard to freedom and independence and debates whether indentured Indo-Caribbean women were free or bonded. Some studies argue that indentured women were "denied freedom",[18] while others claim that indentured service was "a vehicle for emancipation" for East Indian women.[19] While these views are persuasive, this chapter argues that we cannot look at extremes or the binary opposite to determine whether indentured women were free or bonded. The position of women under indenture can be defined in the space between Indian patriarchy at the bottom of the plantation's social structure and the dominance of European imperialist ideology. This can be understood by using various post-colonial theories including Homi Bhabha's mimicry, hybridity and stereotype.[20]

The final section summarizes the consequences of indentured service and concludes that it was perhaps one of the worse acts of humanity against humanity. Despite this, indentured service had important functions: it was a supplier of labour in times of crisis and therefore made up for the deficiencies in the capitalist economy. Indentured East Indians saved an ailing sugar industry in the Caribbean and sustained it long enough so that the right mechanisms were put in place to ensure its survival. But indentured servants were subjected to victimization. Equally important, however, was their capacity to establish protective barriers against complete domination, and they found ways to make indenture beneficial to themselves. Failure to recognize this equation would misrepresent the way indentured servants survived in the Caribbean.

Chapter 1

Migration and Recruitment

The Bases for Indentured Labour

Migration has always been important to the lives of East Indians in India. Despite some caste restrictions, they have migrated in and around India for employment and for religious reasons. But the nineteenth-century movement of East Indians to labour in the Caribbean was directly related to an aggressive imperialist project. From the late fifteenth to mid-twentieth centuries and, in some cases, to the present, Western powers had control over the non-Western world to a point where no part of the globe was left untouched. Much of the non-Western world, which had become known as colonies or the Third World, was a laboratory for testing various theories of colonialism. In this context, the word colonialism means European nations maintaining or extending their control over foreign dependencies or colonies (politically, economically and socially) for raw materials to facilitate the second industrial revolution. In a very strange way, the project of European colonialism spawned some resistance within the European community. By 1840, some of the worst excesses of colonialism, especially slavery, had penetrated the imperial consciousness. Therefore, the search was on to find a solution to the so-called labour shortage in the Caribbean. On the one hand, it was argued that foreign labour was necessary to counteract the effects of emancipation on the labour supply. On the other hand, it was argued that the need for foreign labour was "in keeping with the spirit of the age".[1] These arguments certainly led to the importation of foreign labour. But other questions are warranted. Why weren't Europeans brought (at least in large numbers) to substitute slave labour in the Caribbean? Was it really that Europeans were unable to work long hours under tropical conditions? Caribbean historian Eric Williams writes that the notion Europeans cannot work under harsh tropical conditions should not be taken seriously.[2] The main problem with European emigration to the tropics was that white labour would have led to competition among the white population and encouraged movements towards factionalism and disunity. East Indians were brought to work the Caribbean sugar plantations because they were believed to fit the European philosophy of colonialism (might makes right) and Social Darwinism (the pseudoscientific validity of survival of the fittest). The East Indian population was imprisoned in a cycle of interpretation in which the civilizing mission was at the forefront. Exposure to European overlords, or simply to Western work routine, it was believed, would result in the gradual improvement of East Indians – their manners, taste, morals, opinions and intellect.[3] Such views were already in vogue in India before indentured emigration. The British administrator, Thomas Babington Macaulay (1800–1859), established a school system in India to train the children of East Indian elites so that they would be East Indian in blood but British in taste and mannerism.[4] Within this context, East Indian contract workers were brought to the Caribbean. Their arrival was one segment of a larger population movement. East Indian indentured labourers were also shipped to Africa and Asia to provide labour on coffee, sugar and tea plantations.

Studies of international labour migration have traditionally adopted the perspective that people move because of "push" and "pull" factors generally associated with the markets. Migrants have often been conceptualized as actively responding to crises at home, taking opportunities to fulfil self-interest and trying to exercise control over their own destiny.[5] Although the application of the "push" and "pull" model of international labour migration has been persuasive, it does not adequately explain East Indian indentured emigration to the Caribbean. Prospective emigrants did not act solely in response to conditions at home and abroad. The "push" and "pull" analysis has been used to explain East Indian emigration to the Caribbean.⁶ While these studies have improved our understanding of East Indian emigration substantially, a different and a more sophisticated analysis of such labour migration is long overdue. For a different perspective, one has to examine the expansion of Western imperialism and colonialism in the nineteenth century. Western imperialism is essentially a policy or practice of Western governments to extend their authority over other territory by force for the establishment of economic and political hegemony.

Without a doubt, East Indian emigration in the nineteenth and early twentieth centuries was directly connected with the world capitalist system. Immanuel Wallerstein argues that the world economy is held together by a single capitalist system, and the drive towards capital accumulation internationally operates in a single division of labour with the involvement of myriad policies and cultures.⁷ This process of capital accumulation is supported by a labour surplus drawn mainly from less progressive or less developed areas of the world.⁸ Because of inter-capitalist competition, there is an uneven character of development resulting from centuries of European imperialism, fuelled largely by industrialization in Europe. There were actually two phases of the Industrial Revolution. The first was simply when steam replaced water and wind as a source of energy (specifically in Britain in the 1780s). The end result was a mass production of basic goods and services. The second industrial revolution (1870–1914) emerged when steel replaced iron, and electricity replaced rudimentary forms of power. The development and demand of industrialization acquired an aggressive imperialist character in which various areas of the world were integrated into the Western political-economic system. A metropolitan-colonial relationship subsequently emerged in which the most advanced societies developed systemically at the expense of the less fortunate ones.⁹ For such uneven development of capitalism to function, a labour force had to be maintained and replenished, and workers had to be placed in a position where they subsisted on a hand-to-mouth basis.¹⁰ The colonial mode of economic development during the nineteenth century fits the model of inter-capitalist competition and colonial underdevelopment. The expansion of colonial industries such as coffee, cocoa and sugar and the gradual abolition of slavery perpetuated a so-called labour vacuum in the Caribbean.

The European colonial powers responded to this labour vacuum by moving the labour surplus and unemployed from India to the Caribbean. Terry Repak finds that one fundamental premise of world capitalism is that employers must look for low labour costs or move to where cheap labour can be procured.[11] If employers cannot move, then cheap labour must be imported to support or replace domestic labour.[12]

Inter-capitalist development or the expansion of world capitalism does not simply or singly imply, however, that the sending territory (India) was backward and the receiving territory (the Caribbean) was a flourishing centre. India as a dispatching colony experienced an uneven development because of British colonialism. Foreign penetration and policies of imperialism dissolved the traditional economic and social structure of the countryside, rendering massive population available for labour recruitment. Migration, it was ostensibly believed, would lead to wider opportunities for East Indians and fulfil labour demands in the Caribbean. Under these circumstances, they entered the Caribbean. The demand of the imperialist economy caused internal socioeconomic upheavals in India and promoted East Indian emigration on a large scale.

Even the recruitment process was wholly dictated by external factors. Alejandro Portes maintains that continuous labour migration revolves around the penetration of the political and economic institutions of the dominant society into the subordinate one, which then creates imbalances between the institutions of the subordinate society and eventually leads to labour displacement. These imbalances are induced from the outside and over time become internal to the structure of weaker societies.[13] From this analysis, we can discern that the core of East Indian emigration was conditioned and controlled by particular dimensions of the imperial economy. In this process, they had little or no independent power and were caught in the chains of the colonist command. The forces of colonialism, not choice, charted the course of East Indians overseas. It appears then that the instrumental rationale of their migration to the Caribbean during the nineteenth century can be explained by using the international migration labour theory. The theory argues that capitalist development leads to imperialism, which in turn distorts the development of colonized territories.[14] Because of this world process, a vast majority of Indians were displaced from their traditional economic and social systems, becoming available for emigration. Displaced East Indians became an important source of cheap labour for the development of capitalist-oriented economies.

Conditions Leading to Migration of East Indian Indentured Servants

The Impact of British Colonialism in India

The establishment of British rule in India in 1763 began essentially as commercial ventures, but by the mid-nineteenth century nearly all of India had come under British political and economic control.[15] The demand of the industrial revolution generated an imperial policy which transformed India from a producer of domestic manufactured goods to an international supplier of raw material (mainly cotton) to the British industrial complex.[16] Subsequently, the East Indian social economy and village community systems were altered, and a cash economy was introduced. The ultimate result of British policies in India was that new traders, moneylenders, rent rackers and taxation exacted an enormous toll on the natives. Not only were the natives oblivious to these new developments around them, but vast numbers of them were deceived and indebted in the process. Perhaps even more ominous was that British colonialism demoralized and sapped the spirit and will of East Indian domestic enterprise. Much of British colonialism was supported through a land revenue system in Bengal known as *zamindari* in Bombay and *ryotwari* in Madras. Under this system, the British used the *Zamindar* (lower echelons of the Indian ruling class) to collect revenues from the natives. This system of subjugation generated much confusion, disarray and social conflict which exacerbated the divisions between the privileged and deprived. It is no surprise, then, that the search was on for a new way of linking life with social and economic justice. Nowhere was the effort to eviscerate European domination and forestall the growth of poverty more evident than in the countryside of Bengal, Bihar, Orissa and parts of the Madras Presidency, places where a majority of East Indians were recruited to work in the Caribbean. Droves of East Indians sought to solve their economic hardships by either selling their land or drifting to urban and overseas enclaves looking for employment. Recruiters from emigration firms found displaced labourers quite willing to emigrate in the belief that overseas labour was light in comparison to what they faced at home.

One major cause of international migration is imperialist trading policies.[17] British mercantilist policies strangled the East Indian economy, particularly in rural areas. Mercantilism here means that a nation's prosperity depends on the supply of gold, silver and raw materials from the colonies, and trade is carried out only between the "mother country" and the colonies. Once stable economies, revolving around the production of furniture, embroidery, pottery and silk, found it impossible to compete with British manufactured goods on an equal footing.[18] The structure of the imperial market force crippled local economies, transforming them into new markets driven by new "tastes". Metropolitan goods entering peripheral regions have the tendency to advertise, transmit and inculcate foreign habits of consumption into these areas.[19] Because of this intrusion, peripheral regions are radically transformed and peasants are squeezed out of business and forced off their land, causing distress, displacement and pauperization.[20] Under these circumstances, peasants are often forced to seek alternative sources of survival by moving to other capitalist enterprises, mostly in urban areas. World capitalism did not, however – as in the case of nineteenth-century India – keep pace with rural decline. Not only were alternative jobs hard to find in cities, but basic amenities such as social security, support and welfare facilities that link communities, even in periods of acrimony, were also limited. Thus, the thousands of wandering East Indians looking for employment in urban areas in the mid-nineteenth and early twentieth centuries became potential candidates for emigration. It follows then that imperialism proved to be a vital force in driving potential East Indian emigrants from their homeland.

Socioeconomic Oppression

Concurrent with economic vassalage was socioeconomic oppression. British colonialism did not initiate socioeconomic oppression in India. Instead, it laid the foundation for accelerating and intensifying unequal relationships there.[21] The officiating magistrate of Patna, E.F. Lautour, recounted that in the province of Bihar a sort of slavery existed known as *Kamiuti*: "I have had cases before me on the Civil side which prove the existence of slavery in Behar [*sic*], the lower orders selling their services and those of their children to their Zemindar for any number of years, until the fictitious amount mentioned in the bond is liquidated."[22] Most often the borrower found it impossible to repay his loans – because of high interest rates and other liabilities imposed on him by his capitalist creditor/landlord – and further loans became necessary, creating further indebtedness. As long as loans remained outstanding, the labourer, his wife and his children became bound to the creditor on terms that he and his family might "be whipped openly, sold like chattels, denied rations, leased or mortgaged".[23]

These economic bondages in India were criticized by the British colonial government. British colonial rule sought to put an end to some inhumane aspects of East Indian traditional culture (see chapter 4). But fundamentally, the British realized that even with the abolition of slavery in India in 1843, socioeconomic oppression was too deeply embedded in society for a quick and easy uprooting. The colonial government was content to work with Indian society. The notion of freedom as known in the West, however, was rarely seen in India. What emerged after the British entered India was the intensification of pre-capitalist forms of production relations: backward regions remained backward and stagnant; class and caste oppression increased; feudal relations continued unchecked. For people living in such a state of agrestic servitude, emigration offered an escape from the thraldom of castes and customs, perhaps to begin a new life in a new environment where the circumstances and conditions might be more favourable than what they were experiencing.

Socioeconomic oppression coupled with the effects of imperialism on specific regions in India is not well understood. We can surmise, however, that many could not have survived locally. Kernial Sandhu observed a "vast majority [of Indians] led a hand-to-mouth existence in a chronic state of semi-starvation, or to use a Gandhian hyperbole, in 'perpetual fast'. Life for them was not so much a question of the degree of discomfiture but more a ceaseless struggle just to hang on to the very breath of life."[24] Indeed, these individuals were easily lured to indenture themselves to overseas colonies. A trip to the Caribbean to labour for five years would seem an opportunity to escape from the yoke of helotry, perhaps never to return.

The above data suggest that British colonial rule in India failed to relieve many Indians from the throes of socioeconomic oppression. British rule instead drove most East Indians into the ranks of the penurious. They were tied to their debtors because of limited domestic development and the absence of alternative sources of employment. Capitalist development replaced the functional self-sufficiency of the village system and left many East Indians bound to their landlords and debtors. British colonial programs and policies operated and functioned more with the needs and requirements of their own objectives in mind rather than considering the indigenous social and economic structure of the East Indian countryside. Thus, imperialism, in general, brought the East Indian peasantry into a relationship with the world economy; in particular, the peasantry developed new relationships with the existing stratified social structure. Their low position and bondage to their landlords were intensified and maintained through a more powerful imperial force, making it almost impossible for them to escape their servitude. Eric Wolf notes that capitalism tends to disrupt social customs, "severing people from their accustomed social matrix in order to transform them into economic actors, independent of prior social commitments to kin and neighbours".[25] The continuance of socioeconomic oppression was not merely a matter of East Indian customs alone. Rather, their socioeconomic oppression was due to the economic and political alignment of the power groups which were intentionally designed to serve the colonial authorities and the indigenous propertied castes. The land-owning castes dominated village affairs. All other castes were subjugated to them through employment, loans or sharecropping. The end result was that this relationship was favourable to the landowning as well as the Western capitalist class and caste.

Natural Disasters

The stranglehold on the East Indian rural areas by British colonialism and the unpredictability of the subsistence economy posed serious challenges to the colonial administrative design, particularly in times of natural disasters such as famines and floods. These challenges were handled by actively encouraging and promoting emigration, a move that was influenced by the Malthusian population theory sweeping through Europe in the early period of the nineteenth century. Thomas Malthus theorized that while the population grew geometrically from 2 to 4 to 8 to 16, the food supply only increased arithmetically from 1 to 2 to 3 to 4. If this pattern continued unchecked, then there would be a shortage of food.[26] Thus, emigration was the conduit through which countries could release themselves from the shackles of demographic pressures and increase capital accumulation.[27] Emigration, however, did not bring about an expected transformation of India's population problem except to a small degree in places such as Bengal and Bihar.[28] Emigration as a way of relieving India's population pressure was not practical, at least with regard to the exportation of labourers to the Caribbean "because the colonies wanted able-bodied labourers, not emaciated unfortunates".[29] There was also little significant change in attitude and preference among India's population towards migration, especially among the rural population. Up to the Second World War, 85 per cent of India's population continued to reside in the countryside.

The lack of migration coupled with natural disasters such as droughts, famines and floods in the nineteenth and early twentieth centuries did create some problems for rural India. In southern Asia, the monsoon is a seasonal wind pattern that blows from the Southwest during the drier months and from the Northwest during the wetter months. When the rains are late, thousands starve.[30] Between 1860 and 1908, famine ravaged India at least twenty times, which caused enormous food scarcity, underdevelopment, unemployment and emigration.[31] John Geoghegan, an emigration agent, mentioned that in 1860 and 1861 in the famine-stricken North Western Province, emigration climbed from a mere trickle to 17,899 and 22,000 respectively.[32] Again, J. C. Jha declares that in 1865 and 1866, "when Orissa and Bihar were suffering from terrible famine and scarcity conditions prevailed, in Oudh and the eastern parts of North-Western Provinces 24,571 and 20,109 respectively emigrated".[33] In 1906, the British government emigration agency at Calcutta reported that the "tide appears to be on the turn, as regards to emigration prospects, due no doubt to the drought and scarcity apprehended in the United Provinces, which are our chief recruiting grounds".[34]

On the whole, there was a direct correlation between natural disasters and emigration. For example, in 24 Parganas, Patna and North Shahabad (places where population pressure was high), the number of registered emigrants was high, and in Munger and Gaya (where the population pressure was low), the number of registered emigrants was low.[35] Captain C. Burbank, the superintendent of labour transport at Calcutta, said that even when intending emigrants were rejected as physically unfit for overseas labour, many would stick around the depots merely because of "sheer want" and "scarcity of food".[36] In these times when emigration fluctuated, the restrictions on mobility both from the colonial authorities and from East Indians themselves – particularly with regard to the caste structure and joint-family systems – were less severe. During the regular harvest seasons, emigration was much lower partly because intending emigrants were bound to their immediate surroundings and partly because colonial recruiters found it difficult to recruit East Indians to labour in the Caribbean. The powerful groups in India generally frowned on emigration on the grounds that the "Home Government and other countries" were taking away the available labour.[37] East Indians themselves were emotionally and physically tied to their environment and were disinclined and less disposed to travel.

Civil Wars

Alongside disasters, British colonialism laid the foundation for British military superiority in India. The spirit of revolt and antagonistic feelings against British colonialism in India were always brewing and eventually erupted in the great Sepoy Mutiny of 1857–1858. The Sepoy, derived from the Turkish word *sipahi*, meaning horsemen or soldiers, were native East Indian troops hired by the British. For a long time, the Sepoy served the British army well, but in the 1850s, the British adopted a new rifle for the Sepoy to use. The new rifle was a muzzle loader that used a paper cartridge covered with animal fat and lard. Because the cartridge had to be bitten off and reloaded, it violated Hindu custom – the prohibition of eating beef and pork. Ranks of East Indians in the British army challenged and revolted against this practice. The revolt of these soldiers subsequently caused a great surge of mass migration in which thousands of East Indians fled their homeland to avoid destruction, terror and rampage.[38] The Sanderson Committee – a committee that looked into the affairs of overseas East Indians – reported that the highest total figure ever to emigrate from Calcutta was 27,779 in 1858.

Emigration in India for the same year climbed to 45,838, although the prosperous state of the sugar industries in colonies might have contributed to this movement (pull factors of migration).[39] East Indian rebels (Sepoy) also migrated for fear of being arrested, and thousands chose the Caribbean merely to avoid being sent to Port Blair, a convict settlement established in the Andaman Islands by the British government to imprison the mutineers. Other Sepoys saw emigration as a source of employment.

From the Sepoy experience, it is possible to discern that western military superiority caused the socioeconomic breakdown of East Indian society. According to Lenin:

> Imperialism forces the masses into this struggle by sharpening class contradictions on a tremendous scale, worsening the conditions of the masses both economically – trusts, high costs of living – and politically – growth of militarism, more frequent wars, more powerful reaction, the intensification and expansion of national oppression and colonial plunder.[40]

The nature of East Indian emigration to the Caribbean revealed these dynamics. This emigration was partly buttressed by political unrest, and without it, there would have not been as many incentives for East Indians to work abroad. Political unrest created a pool of unemployed Indians, which the East Indian economy could not absorb.

Personal Reasons and Deception

East Indian emigrants, of course, had reasons of their own for migrating. Some reasons were domestic problems and oppressive personal relationships, family disputes and violation of the law. Others moved because of the spirit of adventure, like the dancing girls who found themselves in Suriname in the 1870s. Considerable documentary evidence, however, has shown that some East Indian emigrants had little understanding of the forces which drove them from their villages. Vast numbers of them were duped and inveigled to labour in the Caribbean. Magistrate H.A. Cockerbell of 24 Parganas informs us that he was aware of "numerous frauds and deception put on the labourer by the recruiter" and many "had been grossly deceived", for which he refused to register them for overseas labour.[41] "The practice of crimping, by men called 'recruiters', to obtain coolies for West Indian and Mauritius labour markets, is carried on with the knowledge and the direct sanction of the government, home and local."[42]

Recent writings have specified that the penetration of capitalism in remote areas of the world for the sake of profits has "significant consequences for the character of labour migration".[43] Much of this impact had to do with Adam Smith's (1776) concept of *laissez-faire* (a French word meaning "leave it alone") and the *Philosophes* (French intellectuals who believed in the concept of applying rational criticism to all things rather than relying on myth and religion) that had emerged around the mid-eighteenth century in Europe. *Laissez-faire* theorizes that the natural law of economics dictates that individuals should be left alone to pursue their own self-interest. All aspects of society would subsequently benefit from the free play of the natural economic forces. In other words, *laissez-faire* embraced the ideals of few governmental restrictions on the movement of goods, capital and labour. Officials in Britain and India nursed and nourished the ideas of free trade and even furthered the free movement of labour internationally. Individual rights and the mobility of labour were sanctioned; in the case of East Indians, they were ushered into the indentured labour system.[44]

The movement of East Indians to the Caribbean became an experiment based on "The Imperialism of Free Trade".[45] The treatment of East Indians in the emigration process was inconsistent with *laissez-faire* and other European ideals expressed during the Enlightenment and in the Bill of Rights. The British administrators in India felt some responsibility for the welfare of East Indian people and to some extent saw East Indian interests as separate from those of Britain. Even though the ideals of the free movement of labour embraced the individual rights of migrants, insufficient attention was paid to the loopholes of the emigration process, which posed serious doubts in the minds of the migrants and the East Indian public. The emigration of East Indians under the indenture system was connected with the imperialism of free trade, and indenture emigration might have gone unchallenged for a longer period, perhaps as long as Caribbean African slavery, had it not been for the migrants themselves, who combated the system. Governmental officials, planters and employers idealized the system of free movement of labour because it benefited them the most. East Indians involved in the emigration movement did not take such a benign view until the impact of the Indian nationalist movement began to be felt from the early twentieth century. Their organization against the system had led to a collective suspicion of emigration among themselves. Therefore, not all East Indians were willing to emigrate.

Factors Discouraging Emigration

Organized emigration from India was never popular in India. Labour recruiters and employers frequently complained about the reluctance of East Indians to move. The emigration agent for British Guiana, Robert Mitchell, observed that an East Indian would not "emigrate while food is cheap. If he can be sure of even one square meal a day, he will not emigrate."[46] Gail Omvedt underlined the home-loving character and the stay-at-home attitude of East Indians against migration in general. She disclosed that between 1881 and 1931, about 3 per cent were involved in long-distance migration, which was cyclical in nature.[47] Most of these movements were for short periods. Long-distance migration and settlement, particularly to the Caribbean, were extremely rare. The main obstacle to long-distance emigration was the concept of *Kala Pani* (black water or the sea). To many nineteenth-century Hindus, especially the high caste, "the terror of the 'kala pani' and the loss of caste [were] only overcome by dire necessity".[48] This assertion might have been exaggerated since East Indians of all castes had been travelling over the high seas for centuries.[49] Nevertheless, the prevailing view in nineteenth-century India was that the moment a Hindu East Indian crossed the black water, his caste was gone, since this act carried the penalty of risking caste defilement and expulsion.

Besides this, there was suspicion among those intending to emigrate that the entire colonial emigration scheme was fraudulent. Emigration agents frequently complained that returned emigrants circulated unfavourable reports which resulted in the "very greatest difficulty in obtaining emigrants for those remote colonies".[50] Many who intended to emigrate assumed that if they indentured themselves to the Caribbean they would be denied wages, converted to Christianity and compelled to eat beef and pork. Brahmans, in particular, were convinced that once they landed in the Caribbean, their holy threads would be taken away. Circulating around major recruiting areas was also the superstition that Indians were taken away to have *mimiai ka tel* (the oil extracted from a coolie's head by hanging him upside down).[51] Stories of an "African King Dahamy . . . [who] was sending parties to catch men for a human sacrifice" because the "government was going to sacrifice the Domes to appease the God of War" were popular in Calcutta.[52] Even among the educated class was the shared view that East Indians were taken away to populate some deserted countries, never to be returned.[53] In addition to superstitious beliefs, cultural factors militated against emigration on a large scale and kept East Indians rooted to their environment. As late as 1921, the Census of India showed caste, language and custom as the main reasons hindering emigration on a large scale.[54]

The possibility of individual emigration was precluded by the notion that East Indians were bound together through traditional family customs (*jati*, a system of extended family) on the same spot for generations. The proportion of the population dependent on the rural environment (agriculture) in the mid-nineteenth century was about 55 per cent. By the end of the nineteenth century, this figure rose to 61 per cent, in 1901 to 66 per cent, in 1911 to 72 per cent and in 1921 to 73 per cent.[55] Furthermore, East Indians displayed an open preference to work in their milieu and to face the hardships they were accustomed to, rather than to venture out to some unknown place under obligations that held great uncertainties.

The treatment of emigrants also discouraged long-distance emigration. Potential emigrants were also averse to migrating because the emigration process paid scant attention to East Indian cultural mores. The typical fault in the recruitment process was that it operated in disregard for the people, their ways, their beliefs; it was simply an insensitive process. For example, by custom and by law, a doctor – a native or non-native – could "examine for venereal rupture, hydrocele and other disorders about the genitals".[56] This practice of examining their genitals was viewed with much disgust and repugnance. Rural East Indians were rarely exposed to Western modes of medical practice, and East Indian women in particular were sceptical about Western medical practice. They often complained of how doctors examined them. Despite these impediments against emigration, a great number of East Indians succeeded in leaving India and established themselves in the Caribbean.

The Emigrant Labourers

Physical Features, Geography, Caste, Language

A majority of East Indian emigrants who came to the Caribbean were single men aged between twenty and thirty years. Fewer families, children and single women came to the Caribbean. Those who came alone carried a low dependency burden with them and were required to return home after completing their terms of contract, especially during the early phase of indentured emigration. East Indians were drawn principally from North and South India and varied remarkably in the area of recruitment – districts, caste and language – throughout the period. During the early phases, between 1838 to the mid-1850s, emigrants were recruited from Chota Nagpur, the present day East Indian states of West Bengal, Bihar and Orissa, and home to the non-Hindu aboriginal tribes: Dhanger/Kol, Santals, Doms, Mundas, Oraons, collectively known as "Hill Coolies" or Jangalis. The hill people's physical features bore a striking resemblance to the African.

> The colour of most Oraons is the darkest brown, approaching to black, the hair being jet black, coarse, rather inclined to be frizzy. [They have] projecting jaws and teeth, thick lips, low narrow foreheads, broad flat noses . . . [their] eyes are often bright and full, and no obliquity is observable in the opening of the eyelids.[57]

Usha Deka believes that East Indians in South India had a history of intermixing with Africans, and that this has "rarely been taken into account in ascribing a Negrito racial strain in this country [India]".[58] This would mean that some East Indians had contact with Africans before coming to the Caribbean, although more research is needed to substantiate this claim. Among the Santals, there lingered a tradition of a *Buru-bonga* (mountain god) to "whom human sacrifices used to be offered, and actual instances have been mentioned . . . of people being kidnapped and sacrificed within quite recent times by influential headmen of communes or villages, who hoped in this way to gain great riches or to win some specially coveted private revenge".[59]

These "hill coolies" lived in the jungle and seldom made contact with peoples from other districts or the lower plains. But, with British colonialism, these tribal people were brought into contact with recruiters to labour in the Caribbean. Being ignorant, timid, hardworking and easily amused, the tribal people were the first to enter the Caribbean via the indentured labour contract system.[60] Their recruitment was never really substantial or regular for three main reasons: (1) the hill people were attracted to the indigo and tea gardens of India, although it was reported that they were being abused by the indigo planters; (2) the voyage to the West Indies resulted in an unusually high death rate, and they were severely maltreated by the West Indian planters; and (3) they believed that the recruitment process involved dishonesty and kidnapping.[61]

By the end of the 1860s, as the hill people dwindled as a source of labour, recruits for the colonies were furnished from Bihar and Bengal. After that period (mid-1870s), colonial recruiters shifted their recruiting operations westward to the North West Provinces (currently known as Uttar Pradesh), Oudh, Fyzabad, Gonda and Basti in the United Province, mainly because of stiff competition from the tea garden recruiters. Except for unforeseen special circumstances in India such as natural disasters and civil unrest, this pattern of emigration continued more or less until the end of the indenture system in 1920.

Besides North India, the main supplier of migrants to the Caribbean came from the sprawling Madras Presidency in South India. Madras emigrants earned a bad reputation for being disinclined to work, difficult to manage, quarrelsome and migratory. Even before the "Madras Coolies" left India, they were posing serious problems for emigration agents at their depot grounds:

> They require entire liberty to come and go as they like and rations on a liberal scale. Any attempt to confine them to their depot grounds, or to interfere with going and coming when they like, will lead to riots, and they moreover distinctly refuse to be accompanied by, or submit to, the authority of the usual Agency Peons. They are as a class addicted to drink and when intoxicated are very violent.[62]

The emigration agent for British Guiana, Mitchell, advised against bringing Madras emigrants to the Caribbean. He stated that although they could "stand the voyage much better than people from Northern India, the death rate at sea barely exceeding three or four in each vessel", they were "not hitherto suited to either of these colonies".⁶³ As a consequence of this perception of Madras emigrants, the recruitment of emigrants in South India was merely a supplementary source to the whole indentured emigration scheme. Caribbean planters preferred emigrants from North India and regarded Madras emigrants not only as inferior workers but also as troublemakers and deserters. Much the same kind of prejudice against this group was noticed in Fiji,⁶⁴ but a less open cultural prejudice against them was apparent in Natal and Mauritius.⁶⁵

A smaller number of emigrants were also recruited from the province of Punjab. Indeed, recruiters found it difficult to enlist Punjabi emigrants to labour in the Caribbean. Being more enterprising and wealthier than other potential emigrants, they had little incentive to emigrate. The colonial government was always wary about Punjabi emigrants and generally instructed against their entry into the Caribbean.⁶⁶ The colonial government, emigration agents and planters preferred emigrants from the agricultural castes, who were likely to be a solution to the Caribbean planter demand rather than a problem. Like the Madras emigrants, Punjabis were singled out as being "undesirables" on the grounds that they were more experienced in the East Indian army. Even though many worked in the fields before they entered the army and were eager to go to the colony for whatever wage offered, they were normally considered by emigration agents as non-agriculturalists.⁶⁷ Only when recruiters experienced difficulties in harnessing recruits from North India did emigration agents turn to Punjab, as was the case in 1911, 1912 and 1913 when Punjabi emigrants were recruited to work for railway construction and irrigation projects in Fiji.⁶⁸

East Indian emigrants were recruited from a wide range of castes. They can be categorized into the four main castes within Hinduism: Brahman (priest), Kshatriya (warriors and rulers), Vaishya (business and agricultural castes) and Sudras (menial castes). On the whole, the caste composition of the emigrants recruited reflected somewhat the caste composition of India, which meant that more low- and middle-caste East Indians were recruited to labour in the Caribbean.

The religious composition of the emigrants also mirrored the religious breakdown of India, with 84 per cent of emigrants being Hindus and 16 per cent being Muslims and other religions.[69] Sociologist Raymond Smith, in a random survey of East Indians entering Guyana between 1865 and 1917, showed among the emigrants 0.1 per cent were Christians, 16.3 per cent were Muslims and 83.6 per cent were Hindus.[70]

The East Indian emigrants brought to the Caribbean an immense linguistic diversity, based on their having been recruited from various geographical regions in India. Missionaries frequently complained about the multiplicity of languages and dialects in the Caribbean and that these characteristics made the conversion of East Indians to Christianity a very difficult process.[71] As expected in a country as large as India, where each region has its own unique historical experience, East Indians spoke, and still do speak, a variety of different languages and dialects, many linguistic groups almost mutually unintelligible. During the indenture period, Trinidad East Indians spoke Bengali, Punjabi, Hindu, Urdu, Oriya, Nepali, Gujerati, Telugu, Tamil, Oraons, Santals, Vanga, Radha, Varendra, Rajbangshi, Magahi, Maithili, Shadri, Awadhi, Bhojpuri, Eastern and Western Hindi, Bangaru, Ajmeri and Tondai Nadu.[72] This linguistic variation was not restricted to Trinidad but was noticed everywhere in the Caribbean where East Indians were indentured.

The occupations of East Indian emigrants before indenture were not as diverse as their caste, religion or language. Although most were agriculturalists accustomed to working under tropical conditions, many were not accustomed to labouring under conditions reminiscent of slavery. Emigrants who were not agriculturalists came from basically two occupational extremes: first, there were Brahmans, Rajputs and Bhojpuri, among others, who had high-level jobs and performed important functions in East Indian society. These emigrants left India because bad times had fallen upon them or just for the sake of adventure. The flow of these emigrants was always small and sporadic. Second, there were emigrants from the "flotsam of humanity", ranging from the landless to beggars to prostitutes. Hugh Tinker states in his classic work, *A New System of Slavery*, that East Indian emigrants who boarded ships to the Caribbean were made up of musicians, cooks, sweepers, coachmen, washermen, grooms and even schoolteachers.[73]

In summary, although East Indian emigrants were drawn principally from North and South India, and were mainly young, single male agriculturalists, they were diverse in language, culture, caste, custom and occupation.

Labour Recruitment

Over the course of the nineteenth and early twentieth centuries, East Indian emigration grew from a small trickle to one of the principal currents in international labour migration. Unlike European emigration to the New World during the same time period, the system of recruiting East Indian emigrants for the colonies was fraught with deception, intimidation and abuse. W.F. Ferguson, the secretary of Landholders' and Commercial Association, was confident that "no Asiatic would prefer seeking employment in a colony, if he knew that to reach it he would have to perform a sea voyage". He warned that if the system continued it would become little more than a "modified slave trade".[74] Three decades earlier, a letter in the *Bengal Hurkaru* newspaper titled "Trade in Coolies" expressed similar views:

> The recent exposure of the mode in which coolies are collected will not admit of a reasonable doubt that natives of this country have been kidnapped and put on board of ships for the purpose of being carried to the Mauritius or other colonies against their will, and have, against their will, been actually taken to the colonies and been compelled to labour.[75]

The same newspaper in another report suggested that the "grand decoy" of East Indian emigrants extended itself from Madras to Bombay and was even practised at more quiet coastal ports in India. These people were shipped and re-shipped from the islands of Bourbon and Mauritius to British Guiana and places unknown. The report added if the "system be not checked, Mauritius will become the slave mart of the East".[76] The *Pioneer of India* called upon the general public and, in particular, the magistrates and police to take into account the "set of scoundrels" who were forcing East Indian emigrants to labour overseas against their will. The newspaper concluded that "some late judicial proceedings have established the fact that the enrolment of coolies for services in the West Indies, as pursued in Allahabad, differs in no essential respect, except one from the old African slave trade".[77]

These reports and voices from several organizations revealed that East Indian labourers were "shanghaied" (an English term originated from the practice of recruiting labourers from the docks and streets of Shanghai by unscrupulous means such as the use of force, deception, alcohol or drugs to work on overseas plantations). From time to time, these views forced the government in India to address the problems associated with the exportation of East Indians abroad. It instituted a combination of laws and sought measures to improve the indentured emigration system. Although these efforts were admirable, they did little to eliminate abuses in the recruiting system because the faults were too deep-seated and beyond radical reform.[78] Being under the direct control of the British government, the Indian government was politically too weak to bring about significant changes to the recruitment process.

India was subjugated to the needs of the dominant British power that essentially transformed it economically into a vassal state.[79] The notion that the government adopted a neutral policy, one that oversaw the fair commercial transactions of East Indian emigrants but was reluctant about getting mixed up in any bargains,[80] needs revision. India, in the nineteenth century, was experiencing the repressive aspects of imperialism. The growth of capitalism as a world system stimulated dominant economies to pull the labour force belonging to weaker economies. The East Indian government lacked precise control over domestic situations, and the recruitment of Indians was laden with grave irregularities. The Sanderson Commission disclosed that the recruiting staff was bad; the recruiters were paid by the results and by the number of emigrants they got, with the consequence that they very often tried to entice married women away from their husbands and tried to get anybody they could.[81] W. S. Wales, the officiating magistrate of Bancobrah, in a letter to the honourable A. Eden, secretary to the Government of Bengal, declared that "all kinds of riff-raff are granted licences as recruiters".[82] Even magistrates were unable to stop crimping and malpractice in the recruitment process.

The Indian government acted appropriately when the most blatant incidents of abuse surfaced, but preferred to deal superficially with the problems of emigration as they surfaced. Between 1838 and 1864, some twenty-one acts were instituted to regulate emigration. Yet loopholes in the indenture system presented opportunities for the laws to be manoeuvred and manipulated. The main difficulty in enforcing government legislation was the powerful force of the capitalist economy, which operated on material rather than human values. The proponents of the recruitment system were merely interested in dividends and not in the general welfare or protection of those who came under their sway. There was a perfect divorce between power and responsibility.

To illustrate how intending emigrants were recruited after the 1864 act was put into practice, consider the following example. In a memorandum to the undersecretary of state for India titled *An Indian Slave Trade*, R. G. W. Herbert, Esq., had this to say about the recruitment of Indian emigrants to the Caribbean:

> A fine-looking woman went out on the morning of the 14th to earn her usual daily wages by grinding corn for a Bunnyah. It appeared, however, that the Bunnyah had no corn for grinding that morning, and she was consequently returning home, when a man accosted her and offered her a job in corn-grinding at six pice [sic] for the day. She followed him to the serai at Kurdabad in the city, where another man made his appearance and demanded her name. She began to suspect something was wrong, and tried to escape, but was hustled into a room in the serai, where a number of other women and a few children were huddled up together, guarded by a third peon. Her entreaties for release were answered by blows and cuffs. She was told not to be a fool, that she would be sent to Jamaica, where she would get Rupees 12 a month besides clothes. She replied that she had an infant at home, and did not want to go away; she was, however, detained, strict watch being maintained over the whole party day and night.[83]

East Indian middlemen kidnapped and lured their countrymen to sign labour contracts in the same way African leaders sold their fellow Africans to European slave traders. Foreigners, however, backed these East Indians. Western powers used "indirect rule" to have control over India and other colonies. The local elites were put in place to carry out colonial objectives (extraction of raw materials, inter alia) in exchange for economic rewards. Sometimes this policy failed, and the local elites were removed and replaced by officials from the mother country (direct rule). The French, for example, used the term "assimilation" to transform their colonial subjects into Western images and "association" to show collaboration with local elites while leaving the native traditions alone. Nevertheless, imperialism played an active role in promoting malpractices in the recruitment of East Indians to labour overseas. Surreptitious recruitment processes were guided by the formula that people of colour from traditional societies were inferior and that their lot could be improved only through labour and discipline, a vile and contemptuous characteristic of imperialism. Individuals from colonized territories (except the ones who accepted the ideals of imperialist assimilation) were defined as biologically and culturally inferior to Europeans, and their local identities were peripheralized and belittled.[84]

The recruitment of East Indian labourers did not revolve solely around the demands and expectations of the planter class. The backing that East Indian middlemen received from foreigners in India and abroad to pursue imperialist needs has been overlooked. Instead, domestic problems in India have been cited or given exclusively for nineteenth-century emigration. There has been a lack of adequate discussion to justify those external factors that promoted internal factors. The growth of capitalism and the way it operated is the key to understanding this. Active recruitment, including the use of East Indian middlemen, was conducted because British imperialism lacked the adequate linkages necessary to make potential emigrants aware of labour opportunities elsewhere or to make their displacement a just cause. Laurence mentions that recruiting agents were sent to scour wide areas in rural India, sometimes several hundred miles inland.[85] Successful recruitment rested upon money advances given to individuals luring them into signing terms of contracts that bound them to the employer. Officiating magistrate of Allahabad I.C. Robertson explains that "it was not uncommon for recruiters to keep coolies for some days in order to run up against them a charge for feeding expenses, in order to hold this threat over them if they show signs of resisting registration".[86] Without this process, the recruitment of East Indians over long distances would have been more difficult and unpredictable. Thus, they, by and large, were manipulated into leaving India to work overseas.

Another example of political manipulation concerned the recruitment of East Indian women. Their recruitment proved a perennial problem for colonial agents. The principal reasons given for their scarcity and the subsequent problems recruiters experienced in dispatching the stipulated number were the planters' preference for a male-dominated labour force and East Indian customs. Families generally shunned sending their wives and daughters to labour overseas. The men usually ventured out to labour with the expectation of returning to share earnings with waiting families. But the difficulty in meeting the quota of female emigrants required cannot be attributed to the planters' preference and East Indian customs alone. The labour recruitment theory implies that employers generally made a concerted effort to cull large numbers of labourers to work overseas. Associated with this effort is the patriarchal aspect of the capitalist system. One fundamental characteristic of world capitalism is that it creates and favours a sexual division of labour in which women and families remain at home while men migrate to job poles. It has shown a preference for a labour force comprising single individuals who will compete against each other for jobs and rely on their own support networks to sustain themselves.[87] This strategy is often successful because migrant workers are generally poor, desperate and tied to pre-capitalist modes of production – in which they are accustomed not only to low standards of working conditions, but they also have little power or exposure to effective organizations (labour unions) to help them. Elizabeth Petras argues that immigrant workers do not have the political clout to assure protection from varying degrees of pressure.[88] Certainly, some of these pressures were noticed among East Indian emigrants in the Caribbean, but whether or not they were the main trends will be the major theme of the next chapter.

1. An unharvested contemporary sugar cane plantation, Skeldon Estate, Guyana

Chapter 2

Domination and Modes of Resistance

Origins of Dominance and Hegemony

The complex as well as diverse factors discussed in chapter 1 that caused the movement of indentured servants to work in the Caribbean are, in this chapter, analysed within the paradigm of domination and resistance. Indentured servants used primary and symbolic actions to resist domination. Their techniques of resistance, especially symbolic actions, were not obvious. These hidden but effective forms of resistance among indentured servants have been overlooked, and their indentured experience has been perceived as a pattern of victimization or as a symbol of social victimhood. However, they were not spineless victims under the indenture system.

A brief discussion of the origin of domination and hegemony and how it has been perpetuated is instrumental in understanding the modes of resistance used under oppressive circumstances. The word domination denotes subjugation, or the exercise of absolute power by a nation, community or individual. Hegemony, on the other hand, signifies predominant influence or leadership. Italian social theorist Antonio Gramsci used these concepts to examine the power structure of European states in the nineteenth century. For Gramsci, domination and hegemony derive from cultural supremacy, which is then legitimized by institutions, including governments. Domination is established through force and maintained through political systems, while hegemony becomes a rule by consent.[1]

Cultural theorist Michel Foucault believes that power comes from discourse, a collection of statements and texts bound together by a common object of analysis and by the particular way this object of analysis is projected. Once a discourse is established, it operates as a self-policing regime, projecting its own domain of truth. Whoever has control of this discourse or societal truth will ultimately have power and, subsequently, determine what should be known and accepted.[2] For instance, if lighter skin is perceived to be better, black and brown skin will have difficulty gaining acceptance. A text purporting such views has the potential to produce a tradition to which governments and academic institutions can adhere. The consequence of all this is that certain discourses produce unequal relationships.

But how were domination and hegemony perpetuated? Nineteenth-century western Europe, in particular, experienced an explosion of growth in the areas of religious freedom, scientific and economic development, and social justice. At this point, it is appropriate to ask why such developments occurred in western Europe and not elsewhere? What was missing in other parts of the world that prevented them from developing as Europe did? It was not so much what other parts of the world were lacking, but rather it was that they did not put certain discoveries – navigation, shipbuilding and weaponry – into practical use. These discoveries, *inter alia*, had taken place in China, India and the Middle East. Europe, however, used these discoveries to dominate the international sea lanes and create vast colonial empires. This period was also an incubation period for the modern world and a launching pad for the era of Western domination that became a reality in the nineteenth and twentieth centuries.

The growing concern for power in western Europe led to powerful governments and stronger economic systems which began slowly to outstrip those of non-Western peoples. By the middle of the nineteenth century, western Europe moved from a semi-backward to a highly industrialized region, helping it to achieve a stunning level of material prosperity unmatched elsewhere in the world. Influenced by the systematic approach adopted by proponents of the eighteenth-century Enlightenment, western Europe entered a new age, embracing notions of the right to freedom and self-determination and placing increased confidence in Western civilization. Renaissance humanism placed human beings instead of God at the centre of the universe. Despite these developments, Europe still found it difficult to keep abreast with the Industrial Revolution and Manichaean delirium. Nevertheless, Europe engaged in the global scramble for overseas colonies for the supply of raw materials, to fulfil the insatiable lust for profits and to achieve a balance of power. Three of many powerful forces or "isms" subsequently emerged – world capitalism, imperialism, colonialism – which subjected the peoples of the non-Western world in unimaginable ways. The world was divided into three zones (core, semi-periphery and periphery) in which two unequal international economic classes (the bourgeoisie and the proletariat) were at the helm. Embedded in these unequal relations was a cultural ideology that promoted racial supremacy like that found in J.A. de Gobineau's *Essay on the Inequality of the Human Races* (1853). This cultural ideology played a pivotal role in assisting western Europe to understand, rationalize and justify the Self/Other dichotomy in order to masquerade superiority, excuse commercial exploitation and bolster imperialism.

The late literary critic and post colonialist, Edward Said, skilfully examined the relationship between Britain and Egypt in the early part of the twentieth century and demonstrated how knowledge and power intersect: "Knowledge means rising above immediacy, beyond self, into foreign and distant lands." In other words, knowledge and power in the nineteenth century meant exploration and conquest. The British used this knowledge to dominate Egypt and "to have authority over it. And authority here means for 'us' to deny autonomy to 'it' – the Oriental country – since we know it and it exists, in a sense, as we know it."[3] As mentioned earlier, this subjugation experienced by Egypt and other colonized territories emerged around the period of European expansion and the Enlightenment. These views were not fully applied to the non-Western world; instead, the West painted a negative picture of the non-Western world with little factual evidence and perpetuated this information mainly because it controlled the configurations of power or discourse. Said writes:

> Along with all other people variously regarded as backward, degenerate, uncivilized and retarded, the Orientals were viewed in a framework constructed out of biological determinism and moral-political admonishment. The Oriental was linked thus to elements in Western society (delinquents, the insane, women, the poor) having in common an identity best described as lamentably alien. Orientals were rarely seen or looked at: they were seen through, analysed not as citizens, or even people, but as problems to be solved or confined, or – as the colonial powers openly coveted their territory – taken over.[4]

By representing the colonized as backward, the West rationalized itself as being scientific and justified treating the colonized world as uncivilized, incapable of governing itself.[5] The West automatically relegated the non-Western world to the basement of the international political and social structure.[6] But this was not all. The West placed itself in a position of intellectual dominance over almost the entire non-European world and appropriated the power to represent and speak for non-Europeans, which eventually gave it the power to conquer, colonize, rule and punish the East as it pleased.[7] Contact with European culture, they believed, would undoubtedly benefit the colonized. Similar statements were repeated throughout the course of Western history. Sir Charles Eliot (1862–1937), a diplomat and an orientalist, in his study of East Indian religion, claimed that Hinduism, the core religion of India, seemed low, foolish and even immoral.[8]

The Western power and domination that epitomized the world in the nineteenth century was also a feature of Caribbean plantation societies. The atmosphere following emancipation provides a good insight into the nature of these colonial societies. There were notable differences between the planters and indentured servants. The planter class were looking for a complimentary and cathartic Caribbean which would guarantee security and stability, while the indentured servants wanted individual financial rewards and, later, familial and community development. Furthermore, two contrasting worlds existed with neither really understanding the other. On the one hand, the planters – whether of a settler or exploiter mentality – brought with them to the Caribbean their imagined "superior ways" and were at the same time quick to dispel native myths and memories as backward and inferior. When they did acknowledge the culture of the Other, it was seen from the perspective of Eurocentric imaginations, which was vaguely benevolent of the local reality. The planter class occupied the great houses and behaved like exiles, longing to retreat back to Europe. They played nobody's game but their own. This behaviour represented imperialist arrogance in its extreme form. On the other hand, indentured servants were sceptical about the planters' judgement about them and struggled to maintain a fairly decent existence in a rigorous and regimented plantation system. One prevailing thought in the nineteenth century was that the steady improvement of the character and habits of people of the non-Western world required continuous contact with the Western world. Towards that end, Western forms of work routine were employed on the sugar plantations and little attention was paid to the culture and customs of the immigrant community.

Subsequently, much of East Indian indentured experience has been depicted in history as a new system of slavery, as slavery in disguise or as a modified system of slavery.[9] A number of studies of East Indians in the Caribbean have followed this model, stating that the indenture system was oppressive to the point of slavery, and East Indians used various stratagems of resistance, primary and psychological, to survive. Kusha Haraksingh writes in *Control and Resistance Among Indian Workers* that on the sugar plantations in Trinidad indentured servants "fostered a general feeling of helplessness; few, if any, of the workers could have believed that a man was the master of his own destiny".[10] The indenture system was routinely oppressive in which the forces of colonialism offered few alternatives but to serve or surrender. Paradoxically, when the cultures of the planter class and the indentured servants are juxtaposed, the planter class is no more complex and no less subjugated, at least in theory, than indentured servants. Both groups were parts of the plantation system, but they were situated at different points, the dominant at the top (planter class) and the subordinate at the bottom (indentured servants). Although they were both enslaved by ideas and behaviour, both classes did not enjoy tangible benefits equally. By looking at the public and hidden transcripts of the planter class carefully, we may discern how the planter class functioned from a position of dominance and power, and we can discover certain techniques indentured servants used to understand how they might have manipulated the plantocracy. Let us now examine the plantation system around the emancipation period in terms of domination and control. This will give us some insight into what indentured servants faced during the initial stages of indentured emigration in the Caribbean.

Domination and Control Around the Emancipation Period

Scholars defined the Caribbean on the eve of emancipation as consisting primarily of plantation societies, which were generally tropical, coastal, coerced and mono-cultural.[11] Plantation societies were also politically hierarchical and class structured in that the major economic institutions revolved around large-scale production and profits. Moreover, they relied on a ready supply of cheap labour to survive. Inequality and subordination were well pronounced. The power structure was shaped like a pyramid with a small white minority at the top and a large black majority at the bottom. The hegemony of the white minority permeated every aspect of society and even extended to dominate the political structure of the state. This group had an inordinate influence on the local culture by perpetuating its supremacy through suppression and subjugation.[12] Eric Wolf and Sidney Mintz argue that plantation societies depended on sufficient capital, availability of large expanses of land, a steady supply of cheap labour to maximize profits, sufficient technology, a disciplined labour force, and sanctions of state power.[13]

Caribbean colonial societies before and after emancipation have always demonstrated a degree of insecurity and instability primarily because they were predominantly male, with an unfree and notoriously coerced majority. Even though these aspects of Caribbean colonial societies were interrupted with the emancipation decree, divisions and exploitation remained the cornerstone of Caribbean political, social and economic life. David Lowenthal points out that, up to the eve of emancipation, the laws discriminated against everyone who was non-white, and the small white minority exercised absolute power over all social institutions.[14] There was little change after emancipation. The ruling class implemented various systems of domination to bind or lock labourers on the plantations.[15] East Indian workers then entered the Caribbean with a restrictive indentured contract system and, more importantly, into an environment where the residue of slavery was still alive. Emancipation was successful in tempering the Caribbean class structure without destroying its hierarchical features. Sugar planters were reluctant to come to grips with the post-emancipation job structure that called for improved housing and better working conditions for menial labourers. They were determined to maintain earlier modes of production and were prepared to make minor concessions to the workers only when pressured to do so.[16] The result was a system that was semi-democratic in form but authoritarian in practice, semi-modern in appearance but traditional in reality. The foci of power remained in the hands of the planter class. This attitude of the planters was an accepted *modus operandi* of Caribbean political, social and economic elites throughout the indenture period. Even though these societies experienced miscegenation, social hierarchy based on skin colour and economic standing persisted and became a cardinal fact of life. The ruling white minority infused in Caribbean society an iniquitous creed that anything non-white was patently inferior and deficient in logical thinking.[17] Even the traces of white blood in other races were considered a deviant and an unacceptable taint.

The institutionalization of power based on the "us" versus "them" ideology has existed in most societies – certainly among the indigenous population long before other ethnic groups entered the Caribbean. There was always evidence of hierarchy within hierarchy, domination within domination. (See the Aztec and Inca civilizations, for example.) But the level and intensity of power relations during slavery and indenture did not originate in the Caribbean. Indeed, the routine of dehumanization, exploitation and humiliation was merely symptomatic of a larger hegemonic force transferred from western Europe to the Caribbean.

The aforementioned analysis of Caribbean plantation societies, during as well as after slavery, underlined the power structure of the dominant class. No one denies or downplays the authoritarian structure of the plantation system in subduing the subordinate classes. But did indentured servants merely accept imposed domination? Certainly, this was not the case under indentured servitude. Many indentured servants resisted domination.

2. *Descendants of the planter class socializing in British Guiana. Courtesy of Skeldon Estate, Guyana.*

3. *A great house, also called the manager's house, at Skeldon Estate, Guyana. Today, the local native manager lives in this house.*

Hidden and Public Transcript

According to James Scott, we can have a substantial understanding of power relations if we examine what he calls the public and hidden transcripts of the dominant and subordinated classes.[18] He suggests that nearly all power relations involve a public and a hidden transcript, which require some acting.[19] Much of what we take for granted – for example, a pleasant smile or a handshake in a contemporary office setting – may be an attempt to conceal innermost feelings in order to get along. Our behaviour may have a strategic purpose because our actions determine how we will be treated in that setting. When large groups of people – indentured servants to the planter class, or slaves to their masters – are routinely subjected to domination over a long period of time, then certain performances and stratagems are essential to their survival.

The public transcript, as Scott describes it, consists of open discourse as well as non-speech acts such as gestures and expressions. In power-laden relationships, the public transcripts of the dominant as well as subordinated classes do not reveal the whole story. Both parties conspire to misrepresent themselves publicly. We might imagine here the public interaction between the master and his slaves. On the one hand, the master might express an amicable gesture to his slaves in an attempt to mask his attitude of dominance or fear. On the other hand, the slave might express deference while concealing his anger. In both cases the public transcript suggests the key roles played by disguise and surveillance in power relations.[20] One striking feature of the public transcript in power relations is that, if the public transcript of the dominant class becomes less transparent or more concocted, the public transcript of the subordinated class will follow suit. Scott again: "If the weak have obvious and compelling reasons to seek refuge behind a mask when in the presence of power, the powerful have their own compelling reasons for adopting a mask in the presence of subordinates".[21]

Ironically, the dominant classes never have absolute control, but their expectations of power generally prevail. One might think of dictators or the Caribbean planters, where power exists alongside uncertainty, instability and insecurity. For domination to prevail, a lot depends on how the subordinate classes conform to power. When the subordinate classes act out (public transcript) what is expected of them, it is believed that the subordinate classes are endorsing their subordination to hegemonic values and are therefore giving legitimacy to domination. It is assumed that the subordinate classes will come to acknowledge and accept their position over time, and moreover, that this process of domination will become justifiable. Certainly, in power-laden relationships, the subordinate classes have good reasons to conform – or appear to conform – to the expectations of the dominant group, especially under slavery. Notwithstanding a few revolutionary movements, the liberty and leverage of the subordinate classes to confront power head-on are severely limited. They have seldom been in a position of strength to exercise any form of reciprocity; that is, to exchange a blow for a blow or a slap for a slap or a humiliation for a humiliation. Even though subordinate classes have supported uprisings like the Mexican Revolution and the Bolshevik Revolution, they have frequently found themselves in an ironic position of having aided power groups whose plans have contradicted the goals they set out to fight for.

The subordinate classes instead engage in sustained efforts not to oppose power. Such sustained efforts – foot dragging, feigned sickness, "playing dumb to know wise" – may fit neatly into the expectations of the dominant class, but they can be misleading. What can be termed in the United States as a form of Uncle Tom behaviour from the subordinate classes may indeed be so, but may also mask true feelings. Similarly, contemporary East Indian labourers in the Caribbean were observed to be obsequious and over-prepared to say "Sahib" to their superiors in order to meet the expectations of their superiors, while maintaining their identity. It would be misleading to suggest that the dominant classes take such behaviour of concealment and manipulation at face value. Throughout history, there has always been a sense of distrust between those who controlled power and those who were subjected to power.[22] Karl Marx and Friedrich Engels argued in their short treatise *The Communist Manifesto* (1848) that the oppressor (*bourgeoisie*, individuals who control the means of production) and oppressed (*proletariat*, individuals who sell their productive labour for wages) have "stood in constant opposition to one another".[23] This distrust leads to formal performance of the public transcript because neither the dominant nor the subordinate class has complete control. Despite its overwhelming power, the dominant class always fears mass revolt.[24]

One might ask how we can distinguish whether the public transcript is authentic or a mere performance. Scott believes that we cannot be sure whether what is said openly is a performance or sincere. He suggests that in order to know the authenticity of the public transcript we have to examine what happens off-stage, behind direct observation, which he has termed "the hidden transcript". The hidden transcript consists of gestures, speeches, behaviours or practices expressed in the comfort zone hidden from specific others. It complements, contradicts or confirms what is often said openly. For the dominant classes, the hidden transcript would be what is expressed in restricted areas such as in special clubs and in social gatherings. This secluded domain allows them to relax from the roles and requirements expected of them in public. The dominant classes have generally been circumspect about overexposure, for they believe that familiarity will breed contempt, and they usually take great pains to present an image that things are "fine". Open disagreements and expressions of insecurities are kept at a minimum and sequestered out of sight. Members of the dominant classes often express their hidden transcript in protected spheres for fear that showing weaknesses and divisions can increase the chances of resistance and outright defiance against them. Beyond the fear of exposure, they have a lot to gain from concealing their hidden transcript. Certainly, they maintain power and, for this to continue, they must make their dominance a legitimate cause. For example, a judge must show that he venerates the law in order to be respected. Likewise, a warrior must act like a warrior, and a king must act like a king. If the public transcript is inconsistent with the ideal image of the dominant classes, then there is a greater likelihood their power base will be threatened.

For the subordinate classes, the hidden transcript consists of suppressing true feelings in the face of power. These feelings are generally expressed behind the backs of the power holders and are revealed in rumours, gossip, folktales, mimicry, rituals, jokes and other modes of subversive resistance. They are essentially acts of disguise in public, concealing critical undertones. The hidden transcript of the subordinate classes is expressed in privileged spheres that represent discourse such as gestures, speeches, practices, ordinarily excluded from their public transcript by exercise of power. It is conceivable, then, that the practice of domination creates the hidden transcript.[25] Consider the hidden transcript of resistance of one black sharecropper in the United States:

> I've gotten along in this world by studyin' the races and knowin' that I was one of the underdogs. I was under many rulin's, just like the other Negroes, that I knowed was injurious to man and displeasin' to God and still I had to fall back. I got tired of it but no help did I know; weren't nobody to back me up. I've taken every kind of insult and went on. In my years past, I'd accommodate anybody; but I didn't believe in this way of bowin' to my knees and doin' what any white man said do. Still, I always knowed to give the white man his time of the day or else he's ready to knock me in the head. I just aint goin' to go nobody's way against my own self. First thing of all – I care for myself and respect myself.
>
> I've joked with white people, in a nice way. I've had to play dumb sometimes – I knowed not to go too far and let them know what I knowed, because they taken exception of it too quick. I had to humble down and play shut-mouthed in many cases to get along, I've done it all – they didn't know what it was all about, it's just a plain fact. I've done played dumb – maybe a heap of times I knowed just how come they done such-and-such a trick, but I wouldn't say.[26]

The words of Nate Shaw reveal how one's true feelings can be disguised in the face of power and domination. They also reveal the rejection of hegemonic values and demonstrate the technique of dealing with social and political domination.

Compliance can also produce a pattern of conformity that appears to accept domination. Such conformity has been most observable in contemporary US prisons where the behaviour of inmates may appear to be compliant when the real purpose has been to use the system to get time off or early release. In the presence of domination, "subordinates appear deferential, they bow and scrape, they seem amiable, they appear to know their place and to stay in it, thereby indicating that they also know and recognize the place of their superiors".[27]

Some studies have suggested that the subordinate classes are adept at observing the powerful because such observation is essential to their survival. For example, a normal day of an untouchable usually revolves around how well he can read his master's mood and how well he can adapt to it. Likewise, the ordinary slave had grown accustomed to practising ritual subservience to his master. Although the suppressed, under the direct wrath of domination, generally train younger ones to conform, this does not mean that they do not have an independent existence. Richard Hoggart, in his study of British working-class culture, finds evidence that, when groups of people feel they cannot do much to change their life situation, they usually "adopt attitudes towards that situation which allow them to have a livable life without a constant and pressing sense of the larger situation".[28] Caribbeanist Orlando Patterson shows that this was historically true for slaves. He argues that the behaviours of slaves in front of their masters were outward forms of interactions, and that we know very little about their individual and group psychology.[29]

The hidden transcript of the subordinate classes, then, represents feelings – anger, aggression, rage – suppressed in the presence of domination. Without the sanctions imposed on the subordinated classes, there would have been more riots, rebellions, revolts and revolutions. As slave narratives have indicated, it is not really the physical sufferings but the insults and the injuries to human dignity that generate the hidden transcript. Furthermore, the oppressed generally have little choice but to watch helplessly as they are ridiculed in front of their spouses, their children and their people. Moreover, they are not in a position to defend their family from such abuse. Much the same sort of ridicule has been noticed among India's large population of untouchables.[30] To understand the hidden transcript of the subordinate classes and how they respond to subordination, an examination outside the earshot of the power holder is required. We must examine the social spheres in which unspoken riposte, stifled anger and bitten tongues created by the imposition of dominance find outlets for expression, areas where domination generally does not reach. Additionally, we must examine social spheres where the voices under domination are expressed, which are not necessarily places beyond the sight of power, but are collective codes of resistance often expressed under the nose of domination. As Foucault points out: "Where there is power, there is resistance, and yet, or rather consequently, this resistance is never in a position of exteriority in relation to power."³¹ The next section will examine how indentured servants used primary and symbolic forms of resistance to manipulate the plantation system to improve their lives.

Primary and Symbolic Resistance

For the sake of convenience, resistance will be categorized into two groups: primary and symbolic. The primary resistance refers to direct defiance such as riots, strikes, rebellion, desertion and acts of revenge. This occurs when subordinate groups have little other recourse for improving their status, diverting suppression and stopping carnage, which Scott aptly calls normal exploitation, normal resistance.³² Symbolic resistance refers to indirect but subversive confrontational struggle against power, including tactics such as foot-dragging, slander, gossip, mimicry, false compliance, feigned ignorance and sabotage. These acts are everyday forms of resistance, which are not obvious. They do not make the headlines of newspapers and other sources of information. Symbolic resistance remains anonymous partly because the dominant group is not interested in publicizing this insubordination and partly because the subordinate group believes that to secure their survival, these acts have to remain unannounced, hidden behind the mask of public compliance. Symbolic resistance is intended to do what Eric Hobsbawn calls "working the system . . . to their advantage".³³ The practice of symbolic resistance requires little co-ordination and little planning, and it is aimed less at changing power relations as at seeking to improve the position of the oppressed.

Primary Resistance Under Indenture

Although the state-fostered authoritarian structure of the indenture system presented an abundance of obstacles against primary resistance, indentured servants did engage in acts of arson, theft, strikes and boycotts.³⁴ Whenever possible, they refused to accept their unjust circumstances. Their routine actions of resistance demonstrated efforts to alleviate and escape the harshness of domination. Frequent quarrels over living and working conditions erupted on the plantations. For instance, on Plantation Eliza and Mary on the banks of the Corentyne River at Skeldon in the early 1870s, indentured servants rioted against unjust wages, as described by one colonial agent: "The subagent attributed much of the ill-will on Plantation Eliza and Mary to recent managers, and to a stricter discipline with regard to continuous work enforced under the new management."[35] Work stoppages were quite common. For instance, Kelvin Singh shows that before the Muharram Massacre in 1884, there were a number of disturbances in Cedar Hill, Trinidad, while in 1889 in British Guiana, D.W.D. Comins recorded twelve strikes.[36] From 1886 to 1889 in the same colony, there were no fewer than a hundred recorded strikes.[37] Indentured servants frequently flocked to the magistrate's office to circumvent and sabotage time and labour.

Some indentured servants injured or killed themselves when the plantation system proved unbearable. The most common self-inflicted injury was suicide through drinking, hanging or drowning, although in Grenada indentured servants swallowed dirt and developed *ankylostomiasis* (a disease that causes puffy face, flabby tongue, waxy complexion and a slow, laboured walk) to show that they were utterly unfit to work. From 1886 to 1890, there were twenty-eight cases of suicide in British Guiana. The same pattern was observed in East Indian communities in other parts of the Caribbean. What is so interesting and ironic about self-inflicted injuries and suicides is that it reveals a core psychological dynamic of resistance. Killing one's self was seen as an act or blow against the plantocracy, against the planter's property and profit.

Another form of primary resistance was desertion. The planters instituted the pass system to restrict the movement of East Indian indentured labourers. Each indentured labourer was required to carry a pass at all times. Violation of this regulation was often punished with fines, imprisonment and flogging:

when estate ork done	when estate work was finished
free	free
if, i gwine neddar estate	if I have to go another estate
white man must gi me pass	white man must give me a pass
without pass pass gwine	without the pass
de fellar go lock e up.[38]	I would be locked up in jail.
	(author's translation)

The system of indenture gave the planters complete control over the time and labour of indentured servants. But this was never tantamount to complete restriction or social death. These labourers were able, within constraints, to manipulate the system to their advantage.

In pre-colonial and colonial Southeast Asia, peasants migrated as long as there were opportunities to do so instead of risking open confrontation.[39] Much the same attitude was observed among East Indian indentured servants in the Caribbean. In the initial phase of the indenture system, labourers dealt with repression by using their right to commute from one plantation to another with the hope of finding better treatment and better wages. When commuting was no longer an option by the 1860s (owing much to the planters' control of the legislature), desertion became a viable alternative to confrontation and repression. One significant theory about power-laden relationships is that the oppressed most often choose flight instead of confronting domination head on.[40] This behaviour can be seen to be guided by the Reactance Theory that posits there is a fundamental human desire for freedom and autonomy which, when threatened by force, leads to the need to restore freedom.[41] Thus, the frontier character, especially of the Guianas, induced East Indian labourers to defect. From 1881 to 1890, it was calculated that about 517 indentured servants each year deserted the plantations in British Guiana.[42] In French Martinique, desertion climbed from thirty-seven in 1862 to 704 in 1884,[43] while in Jamaica the number of desertions was 380 from 1910 to 1921.[44] Brian Moore notes that indentured labourers from British Guiana decamped to Venezuela, Suriname, Trinidad and French Guiana in what Alan Adamson believes were hopeless efforts to reach India.[45]

Deserting indentured servants were never successful in developing runaway communities like the Maroons in Jamaica and in Suriname during slavery.[46] Many deserters became vagrants wandering aimlessly in the countryside and begging in urban areas, ultimately dying from sheer starvation.[47] The more enterprising deserters worked for interior Amerindians, the Venezuelan cocoa estates, the small East Indian landowning class and the gold industry.[48] Some East Indians escaped from Martinique and Guadeloupe and worked for the British planters in Antigua.[49] According to one source, "secret companies existed whereby a coolie could buy papers showing his indentureship necessities from the granting company and turn his papers over to them which they would reinvest with another coolie".[50]

Primary resistance by indentured labourers prompted further repression from the plantation authorities. Laurence recognizes "a strange paradox in the fact that the people who were so violent and volatile as to seem a grave threat to law and order were nonetheless stereotyped by the planters as a 'docile' labour force".[51] Although the indenture system did not carry the depressing excesses of coercion as in slavery, there were everyday repressions backed by pass and vagrancy laws, rigorous work routines, detention, occasional floggings, and so forth. Scores of reports have indicated that the basic needs of indentured servants were systemically ignored, and great misery prevailed on the plantations. According to one report, indentured servants were forced to work in the gold mines or in the placers in French Guiana with little protection.[52] The acting immigration agent in Martinique witnessed eleven patients, one of whom was lying down on his back on a platform shackled by the ankle to an iron bar. The man was not an invalid, but was treated harshly because he was "suspected of having stolen some rice".[53] Indentured servants in Suriname suffered similar fates. According to India Emigration Proceedings of 1874: "The sickness among the immigrants has been principally chronic dysentery, fever and general debility engendered by abstaining from proper nourishment; also ulcers caused by any small skin wound are very prevalent, and unless immediately attended to mortification ensues from which few recover."[54]

Primary resistance did not change the fundamental basis of domination. Primary resistance certainly threatened the system and forced the dominant classes to renegotiate relationships, but the substance of the power structure remained virtually unchanged. Several factors explain this phenomenon. East Indian indentured labourers were in the Caribbean on a contractual term and never conceived their stay as permanent. Many indentured servants feared that if they fought against the system, they would prolong their contracts and forfeit their entitled return passage to India.[55] Furthermore, the indenture system was not always as openly repressive as slavery, so there was less incentive to resist. The indenture system was at times favourable to East Indians with regard to offering them parcels of land and fringe benefits, which they would have been unlikely to acquire had they remained in India. A majority of indentured servants worked the system to finish their contracts and to return home.[56]

The indenture system was not so oppressive that it destroyed all vestiges of independent social life. Like serfdom and sharecropping, indentured service allowed East Indians to construct a social life and culture without total control by the dominant class. Since the goal of the indentured servants was never to overthrow or to transform the system of domination, they tried to survive day to day, week to week, season to season – within the system. Karl Marx calls this situation the dull compulsion of economic relations.[57] When peasants lack the opportunity to change their position, they do not seek to redress their situation but adjust to it as best they can. Like Marx, Emile Durkheim suggests that human beings are forced to act and behave in certain ways regardless of their preferences and expectations.[58] Individuals accept certain working conditions, even though they may be genuinely displeased with what they do, because they do not have the means to alter their working conditions on a short-term basis.

Primary resistance requires an element of self-control in the face of domination. We have seen this self-control expressed among subordinate groups, and one striking example has been among black men in the United States. Lawrence Levine's study of the Dirty Dozens in *Black Culture and Black Consciousness* shows how black men in pairs traded rhymed insults against each other's family (especially female members), with victory being achieved by not losing one's temper, but rather by devising clever insults in a pure verbal duel.[59] "Developed at a time when black Americans were especially subject to insults and assaults upon their dignity to which they could not safely respond, the Dozens served as a mechanism for teaching and sharpening the ability to control emotions and anger; an ability which was often necessary for survival."[60] There is evidence that indentured servants adopted similar styles of resistance on the Caribbean plantation. Thus, for us to know how indentured servants resisted domination, we need to examine their sites, their comfort zones, where they were free to express themselves. Their private environment offers us the opportunity to examine the hidden transcript, the symbolic and cultural forms of resistance of indentured servants against domination.

Symbolic Resistance Under Indenture

When Derek Walcott accepted the Nobel Prize in Literature in 1992, he began by making references to the Trinidad/East Indian village of Felicity, where he had once seen the East Indian festival of *Ramleela*, a dramatization of the Hindi epic *Ramayana*. Walcott admits he was misreading *Ramleela* as a mere play rather than a faith, as the following quotation suggests:

> Multiply that moment of self-conviction when an actor, made-up and costumed, nods to his mirror before stopping on stage in the belief that he is a reality entering an illusion and you would have what I presumed was happening to the actors of this epic. But they were not actors. They had been chosen; or they themselves had chosen their roles in this sacred story that would go on for nine afternoons over a two-hour period till the sun set. They were not amateurs but believers. There was no theatrical term to define them. They did not have to psych themselves up to play their roles. Their acting would probably be as buoyant and as natural as those bamboo arrows crisscrossing the afternoon pasture. They believed in what they were playing, in the sacredness of the text, the validity of India, while I out of the writer's habit, searched for some sense of elegy, of loss, even of degenerative mimicry in the happy faces of the boy-warrior or the heraldic profiles of the village princes. I was polluting the afternoon with doubt and with the patronage of admiration. I misread the event through a visual echo of History – the cane fields, indenture, the evocation of vanished armies, temples and trumpeting elephants – when all around me there was quite the opposite: elation, delight in the boys' screams, in the sweets-stalls, in more and more costumed characters appearing; a delight of conviction, not loss. The name Felicity made sense.[61]

Walcott was not the only one to have misread East Indian culture in the Caribbean. He merely expressed a misconception held for centuries there. During indenture, the planter class perceived East Indian culture as ancient and alien to Western traditions, only attracting attention when its customs interfered with the general routine of plantation labour. In the daily run of things, indentured servants were seen as largely illiterate, speaking various unintelligible dialects, living a life of their own. Perhaps it is this negligence to which Walcott refers that allowed East Indians to maintain pivotal aspects of their culture in a conflict-habituated plantation complex. Walcott's speech reveals how the hidden transcripts of *Ramleela* in the Caribbean survived the rigours of the indenture system and became a public transcript.

The indentured servants relied on their own solipsism and cultural resilience – in forms of feast and festival – (*Divali, Phagwa,* fire-walking, stick-fighting, *Hosein, Eid-ul-Fitr, Shiva-Ratri*) to deal with the coercive regimen of indentureship. This cultural resilience appeared in drama, dress, ritual, religious beliefs and so on. Their distinctiveness, as in the case of *Ramleela*, was created in large part through determination because, as Walcott tells us, "they believe[d]" in what they were doing. Indentured servants chose certain cultural expressions and practices to meet their perceived needs, while at the same time they were reluctant to accept or understand Western ways. The dominant culture was inconsistent with their expectations and therefore was believed to be less valuable to them. Eric Hobsbawn points out that the mere refusal to understand represents a form of class struggle.[62] The indentured servants did not accept the cultural mores and status of the ruling class. Their reluctance to accept the dominant culture fully proved to be more of an asset, creating codes of resistance – patterns of appearance and expression – known only to them and inaccessible to the group it was intended to exclude. Scott writes that "[a]lternatively, the excluded (and in this case, the powerful) audience may grasp the seditious message in performance but find it difficult to react because that sedition is clothed in terms that also can lay claim to a perfectly innocent construction".[63]

When policed or pushed into conformity, indentured servants came to rely on their own symbolic resistance and primordial aspects of community and religion, which the dominant classes neither understood nor sympathized with. Nowhere has this misreading and misinterpreting of cultural resistance and adaptation been more evident than in Kelvin Singh's study *Bloodstained Tombs: The Muharram Massacre, 1884* and in Chandra Jayawardena's study of ideology and conflict in three Guyanese plantations. In the first case, Singh shows how the annual Muharram or Tadja celebration "provided a social bridge to the rest of society" in Trinidad. Muharram occurred on the first month of the Muslim year which commemorated the death of the Prophet Mohammed's grandsons, Hassan and Hussain, in the seventh century. The festival was celebrated by Muslims, Hindus and Africans because it was a flexible arena for interracial, interethnic and interreligious participation. The festival proved to be a fertile ground for cultural and national integration. But, on 30 October 1884, the colonial police shot dead at least sixteen East Indians in an attempt to deter them from practising their custom and culture openly. Despite these mindless killings, which became known as the Muharram Massacre of 1884, and despite the fact that in some areas in Trinidad the festival was abandoned, the annual Muharram celebration continued. The celebration provided an emotional release for indentured East Indians. Noted Kelvin Singh:

> For most Hindus, who constituted the majority of the Indians in Trinidad, the Muharram offered at least one day in the year on which [they], like their Muslim brethren, could find cathartic release from the monotony of labour and confinement on the plantations. It was also an occasion on which bonds of social solidarity with their Kith and Kin on the other plantations could be reaffirmed, something about which the colonial ruling class was to become apprehensive in the early 1880s.[64]

In the second case, Jayawardena indicates that resistance against domination requires solidarity and even some degree of conflict. But conflicts should not be seen as evidence of disunity and weakness. They may be signs of unity. Jayawardena states that indentured servants developed strict egalitarian social relations through *Mati*, a solidarity adopted while in transit to the Caribbean.[65] Alongside *Mati*, there were collective outbursts among themselves and against the plantocracy with no identifiable leadership, although Clem Seecharan has shown that the spirited leadership of indentured Bechu has been overlooked in Indo-Caribbean historiography.[66]

Mati was preserved in spite of attempts from the management to infuse the concept of divide and rule among the workers. Solidarity was maintained because *Mati* was designed to prevent the growth of internal differentiation in rank and income that usually creates divisions in communities. Unity among indentured servants was possible because

> if the high incidence of disputing is related to the acceptance of an egalitarian ideology that enables a peasant to identify his interests with those of his fellows and to recognize a common fate, then one can understand the source of long-run cohesion and stability, despite the many disputes arising from the incompatibility between the ideology and individual differentiation.[67]

Jayawardena shows, then, that disputes among Guyanese plantation workers – violation of *Mati* through efforts from the management, personal disputes, court cases and so on – did not weaken them but rather indicates strong bonds of community. Thus, it would be misleading to assume that domination from the ruling class and disputes among East Indian plantation workers were signs of disunity and weakness. It would be more accurate to assume that disputes among the Guyanese workers created possibilities for resistance and accommodation.

Members of the dominant class, more often than not, live and die among their subordinate classes and know very little of their character. The dominant classes behave one way in front of the subordinate classes and another way among themselves. Little wonder, then, that the indentured servants created distinct and discrete polyglot subcultures and sub-communities in the Caribbean. It was a sort of a social movement in which they organized and orchestrated life into the manifestations of their own codes, heroes, myths and social standards in spite of tremendous odds:

> Deprived of their original language, the captured and the indentured tribes created their own, accreting and secreting fragments of an old, epic vocabulary, from Asia and from Africa, but to an ancestral, an ecstatic rhythm in the blood that cannot be subdued by slavery or indenture, while nouns are renamed and the given names of places accepted like Felicity village or Choiseul.[68]

The planter class tried hard to create disunity among the immigrant labour groups so that a collective hidden transcript would not be developed and disseminated among them. During slavery, the planters brought to the Caribbean Africans of greatest linguistic and ethnic diversity. The aim was to minimize communication and unity among Africans on the premise that this would inevitably lead to rebellion. The planters reasoned that free communication would imbue in Africans a false notion of equality and make them intractable. This policy interestingly led to the development of a Caribbean dialect of Pidgin that was unintelligible to the planters. Efforts were subsequently made to have Africans converse in languages the planters would understand, especially at the work place.

The arrival of indentured servants from India further frustrated communication. Their multiplicity of languages and dialects such as *Sarnami* in Suriname, which were never before heard in the Caribbean, added a new dimension to communication on the plantations. The planter class, of course, embraced their one language, one cultural way of life, and tried to subdue any developments inconsistent with the routine of plantation life.

When this strategy proved ineffective, the planters denigrated and directed encrypted discourses at East Indian languages and dialects. These methods of control, however, were not successful in preventing the development of unique linguistic codes, which were instrumental in facilitating and forging a symbolic sociological solidarity among indentured servants. They did not have to resist domination in their spheres of comfort but directly under the nose of domination, since the planter class scarcely understood what they were saying. Paradoxically, the planters aided this process. The planters' attitudes of inhibition and avoidance towards East Indian languages inadvertently limited their liberty of control, which played into the expectations of indentured servants. The foci of power were decentralized without being confronted head on. This linguistic metonymy was one of many unforeseen aspects of resistance and accommodation that epitomized the experience of indentured servitude. For instance, even the children of East Indian indentured servants, not to mention the Caribbean society at large, did not understand the linguistic communication of their parents and grandparents. Older Caribbean East Indians still discuss problems and issues in front of family members without the latter knowing what is being said. They also engage in code-switching, that is, the process of changing from one level of language to another as the situation demands, whether from one language to another or from one dialect to another. It is interesting to note that apart from this technique, which presumably developed during the indentured period and was handed over to subsequent generations, code-switching generally emerged from the inequality of languages or the perception of inequality of languages. There is, however, a value and a sense of identity and reason for its persistence. This was certainly the case under the indenture system.

Apart from the use of language, indentured servants engaged in gossip as symbolic resistance against the plantation system. Gossip is the most familiar strategy used against domination. It includes character assassinations, rumours and nicknames, intended to chip at the reputation of and respect for the power holder. Gossip involves a story of some sort told about a third party who is not there. The author or leader is not clearly recognized, but once the story is launched it can spread like wildfire. The subordinate groups use gossip because it "achieves the expression of opinion, of contempt, of disapproval while minimizing the risk of identification and reprisal".[69] Gossip reinforces standards among subordinate groups as to what should be mocked, despised and disrespected. Generations of East Indian children grew up listening to gossip and stories of British idiosyncratic colonial experience in the Caribbean. In rural Guyana, for example, meals on wedding days, feasts or festivals are generally served on a large round leaf instead of a plate, as expressed in Roy Heath's *The Shadow Bride*: "The immense yard of beaten earth, strewn with raised concrete squares for threshing paddy, was filled with guests who stood around or sat on stools while consuming rice and mutton served on plantain leaves."[70] As the story goes, the British guests began to eat the leaves they were given before the meals arrived. Many of the natives watched with utter surprise, especially since the leaf was bitter, then broke into laughter.

The symbolic meaning of this storytelling is no different from seeing the lion being chased by a goat or a fox being chased by a rooster. In the presence of domination, nothing more fulfils the desire of the subordinate classes than to see the oppressor confused, fooled and outwitted. The reversal of roles presents an escape and even a victory, but importantly, it shows how the weak learn ways to deal with the more powerful. The mere opportunity to see the powerful being ridiculed creates a feeling of superiority on the part of the storyteller and his audience. It strengthens the sense of group cohesion and develops communal consciousness and solidarity.

Indentured servants also used humour to resist the repressive aspects of the plantation system. Sigmund Freud described the function of humour in power-laden relationships as "the triumph of narcissism".[71] According to Freud, humour is not silenced; it is counteractive and signifies the strength of the ego, which refuses to be hurt by any insidious forces. "Humour is not resigned; it is rebellious. It signifies the triumph not only of the ego, but also of the pleasure principle, which is strong enough to assert itself here in the face of the adverse real circumstances."[72] Freud illustrated this process by using a joke of a condemned man on his way to the gallows. The man's last words were: "Well, this is a good beginning to the week."[73] He believed that jokes like these were intended to make the person impervious to pain; and, in this example, the condemned man was adopting an attitude of an adult towards a child.

It is this: that the one is adopting towards the other the attitude of an adult towards a child, recognizing and smiling at the triviality of the interests and sufferings which seem to the child so big. Thus, the humorist acquires his superiority by assuming the role of the grown-up, identifying himself to some extent with the father, while he reduces the other people to the position of children.[74]

A good deal of contemporary laughter, like the "ghost is always white" and other jokes in Caribbean East Indian communities have given us some insight into how servants symbolically resisted the indenture system. The following is a dialogue between a member of the dominant class and a young indentured servant:

> Massa asked what is that in the tree beside those delicious mangoes?
> The Indian boy remarked, pay-see/chay-see, Massa
> I will go and get some mangoes, Massa said
> Massa went up the tree and picked the mangoes but touched the pay-see/chay-see,
> And Massa rushed down the tree
> The Indian boy asked, wha happen, wha happen Massa?
> Why the hell didn't you say that pay-see/chay-see are stinging bees?[75]

To cite another example: discovering red, round hot peppers for the first time, the white folks were told they were cherries and paid an exorbitant price for them both in money and in taste.

Studies on how East Indian indentured servants used laughter and humour to resist domination are rare. There is a substantial body of literature on black laughter in the United States during and after slavery. American blacks used laughter to deal with their oppressive conditions and to exert some degree of control over their environment. Much of the same sort of laughter has been noted among black South Africans to fight racism and among the Japanese to mock conformity in their society.[76] Humour is a form of reality play which is a product of reality construction. It comes from the contrast between two different realities. The first reality is conventional, that is, what people expect in specific situations; the second is unconventional, an unexpected violation of cultural norms. Humour arises then from contradiction, ambiguity and double meanings found in the differing definitions of the same situation.[77] Freud saw laughter as a release of psychic or nervous energy. He claimed that in joking, the energy saved is that which would ordinarily be used to repress hostile or sexual feelings and thoughts. Joking (like dreaming) serves as a safety valve for forbidden feelings and thoughts, and when we express what is inhibited, the repressed energy is released in laughter.[78] This laughter is classified as the relief theory and "goes back to Aristotle's comment on catharsis in comedy".[79] If the relief theory is correct, laughter and humour on the plantations would "take up the slack between the momentousness of the situation and the feebleness of those in the situation by *dwarfing the situation*".[80] Laughter and humour did not change the physical situation on the plantations, but it lightened the burden and monotony of plantation life and added some joy to the existence of indentured servants. It was the perspective through which indentured East Indians understood their situation, released their inner suppressed feelings, diverted their sufferings and accommodated their hardships without losing their identity.

Chapter 3

Cultural Change and Continuity: Caste and the Joint Family Systems

Theories of Cultural Change

The previous chapter established the importance of primary and symbolic resistance for indentured servants to deal with the exigencies of plantation life. They understood the power structure of the dominant class and manipulated it to better suit their needs. This chapter extends the argument that indentured servants were not merely victims of the indenture system. Cultural change, whether forced or voluntary, helped them to acquire a better status in the Caribbean than in India. Cultural continuity also helped indentured servants to experience intergenerational socioeconomic mobility. Strong family and communal bonds were continued through conscious motivations.

Social scientists have always been interested in how some cultures experience continuous change in response to shifting demands in their environment, while others retain certain cultural traits with constant, reaffirmed identities. The evolutionary and interactional models of change and continuity have been used to explain this process. The former examines change and continuity on the broad and specific levels of human development, arguing that society goes through unilinear and multilinear changes. The evolutionary model states all societies follow the same path of change, from simple to complex forms (savagery, barbarism and civilization), while the interactional model states that all societies follow different routes that emerge at the same stage of development.[1] This latter model examines change under particular circumstances in the human population.[2] As societies move from traditional to industrial stages, family patterns also change from extended to the conjugal types with stronger emphasis on the nuclear family. The process of change is complex and varies from society to society, but fundamentally, while changes in families may be profound, changes between contiguous generations may be minor, leaving core attitudes and behaviour intact.[3]

Researchers have been particularly concerned with attempts by the plantation system to isolate Caribbean societies from their old cultures and yet how these societies were able to maintain certain aspects of these cultures in a hitherto unknown environment. On the one hand, it has been argued that slavery caused a severe rupture between Africa and Caribbean societies, which created newly truncated cultures in the Caribbean.[4] On the other hand, it has been argued that African Caribbean societies retained, reinterpreted and adapted West African cultural forms. Africans in the Caribbean held on to their core cultural beliefs such as animism, folklore and myths, in spite of the pressure to acculturation.[5]

This debate has spawned other theories. The most influential has been the Plural Society Theory. Jamaican anthropologist, M.G. Smith, argues that in plural societies each group maintains its own culture, religion, language and so on. These groups live side-by-side and mix only when it is necessary, for example, in the market and workplace.[6] There is no consensus in these societies, which are marked by conflict and instability and yet are united by force imposed from the top. As a result, they do not necessarily experience hybridization – a process whereby separate or different practices combine to form something new. Rather, these societies experience multiculturalism – the respect for differences rather than assimilation into one dominant culture (the "salad bowl" as opposed to the "melting pot" phenomenon).

Smith's concept of pluralism had been met with much criticism. Raymond Smith and Lloyd Braithwaite (following Talcott Parsons's Action

Theory – which was influenced by the work of Emile Durkheim and Max Weber) claim that although Caribbean societies are divided racially and socially, they are nevertheless held together by a set of shared or foundational values that emerged from a common plantation experience.[7] These societies are more culturally integrated than culturally diverse. Later studies have pointed out that these societies have experienced creolization, a term that explains the acculturation and interculturation of African and European cultural forms in the Caribbean. Creolization has also been critiqued by scholars in multiethnic societies like Guyana, Trinidad and Suriname for being insensitive to the maintenance of East Indian traditional cultural ways. Ralph Premdas argues that it can be dangerous to designate ascribed collective identities, because it can assume hegemonic cultural claims that malign or marginalize other cultural groups.[8]

Earlier debates on the African school of cultural change and continuity have been used to explain East Indian experience in the Caribbean. Joseph Nevadomsky has argued that while Indian emigrants did not arrive *tabula rasa* ready to incorporate themselves in the Caribbean, their culture experienced continuous structural change, especially in education,[9] social life,[10] language[11] and caste.[12] He writes that the East Indian family was not able to maintain its integration as a traditional system in the face of social change. Many East Indian customs, especially the caste system, barely survived the indenture system. Those customs that did survive were faced with the consequences of continuous social change and development in rural communities. As a result, new patterns of integration have developed in East Indian communities.[13]

By contrast, Morton Klass has affirmed that East Indians in the Caribbean maintained some important homeland social institutions such as marriage and joint family patterns with some modifications. Obviously, it was not possible for East Indians to maintain exactly their ancestral culture. Their home life and some private affairs, however, remained the same; their social location changed, but some aspects of their non-material culture remained. East Indians were individual carriers of their own culture through their strong family institutions and values, especially in the face of pressure to change.[14] Niehoff has claimed that despite the great disadvantage the East Indian family experienced in Trinidad, it stood apart from other ethnic groups in that it retained a remarkable degree of Indianness.[15] Much of this cultural persistence and retention had to do with the plantation policy of rural isolation and neglect that began under the indenture system.[16] Rural development and educational opportunities were limited in East Indian communities.[17] Subsequently, some basic forms of Indian life – marriage customs, rarity of divorce, unequal status between men and women – were not truncated but transplanted to and retained in the Caribbean.

Caste and Cultural Change

Of all East Indian cultural institutions, the caste system – and, in particular, the position of Brahmans – experienced the most significant changes in the Caribbean. Caste is an enclosed form of social stratification wherein status is determined by birth and is unchangeable. Individuals are born to stations of life with no opportunity for social mobility. Status cannot be achieved; it is ascribed. Boundaries between castes are firm. It is believed that the Aryans (the word *Arya* means tiller of the soil) from Europe brought the caste system to India and used it to separate themselves from the darker Dravidian races and aboriginal tribes. According to Benedict, the caste system in India has some common characteristics: (1) ascription by birth, (2) endogamy, (3) hierarchy, (4) occupational specialization, (5) religious restrictions on social interaction, and (6) some interactions of caste groups at least on a local level.[18] There are thousands of castes and sub-castes (*jati*) in India. Caste, however, is traditionally ranked within four *varnas*: Brahman, Kshatriya, Vaisyas and Sudras. Beneath these four *varnas* are the untouchables. Senart describes the caste system as follows:

> The Brahman's only duties are to study and teach the Vedas, to offer sacrifices, and to offer, and above all to receive, gifts. It is the duty of the kshatriyas to give orders, to protect the people, to offer sacrifices through the medium of the Brahmans and to study the Vedas; the Vaisyas must raise livestock, cultivate the soil, engage in trade and give alms, not neglecting either the sacred rites or the study of the written word; Sudras have only one essential task – to serve the higher castes. Outside this system there are only barbarous or despised peoples who have no access to the religious and social life of the Brahmanic world.[19]

In Hinduism, the caste system is part of the social body. The heads of society are the intelligent, priestly Brahmans, the advisors. Then there are the arms of the body, the Kshatriyas, who act as defenders and administrators of the communities. The Vaisyas are the stomach of society, acting as providers. The Sudras are the legs and feet of society, supporting the three other castes in service. Central to Hinduism and Indian life in general is the concept of *Dharma* and *Karma*. The former is a set of laws that set the behavioural standard for all individuals in Indian society. It is the obligation and discharge of one's duties to oneself and to others. The latter, *Karma*, is a Sanskrit word meaning deed and comprises the entire cycle of cause and effect and is the sum of all that an individual has done and is currently doing. The effects of those deeds actively create present and future experiences, thus making one responsible for one's own life. Another tenet of Hinduism is *Maya* which means illusion, a deep conviction of the Hindu mind that the material mind is illusory. The caste system operates with no competition between castes. Only the dominant caste has an autonomous existence.[20] The upper castes generally resist upward mobility of the lower castes, especially the untouchables, sometimes through violence.

Most East Indians who came to the Caribbean were also from the low and middle castes, but a sizable number of them were also from the high castes. Table 3 shows the castes to which these emigrants belonged in the Caribbean during the 1870s.

Table 3: Castes of East Indians in the Caribbean in the 1870s

Caste and Religion	British Caribbean	French Caribbean	Dutch Caribbean
Hindus, Brahmans, High Castes	1,454	410	514
Agriculturalist	3,281	799	1,012
Artisan	875	292	255
Low caste	4,951	1,249	1,158
Muslims	1,845	467	580
Christians	28	1	4
Total	**12,434**	**3,218**	**3,528**

Source: India Office Records, *India Emigration Proceedings: Annual Reports of the Protector of Emigrants at Calcutta for 1873–1874* (December 1874), no. 1, 363.

For Trinidad, Brereton shows that Brahman and other high castes were 18 per cent; artisan, 8.5 per cent; agricultural castes, 32 per cent; low castes, 41.5 per cent.[21] For Guyana, Smith suggests that high castes were 13.6 per cent; artisans, 8.5 per cent; low castes, 31.1 per cent.[22] For Martinique and Guadeloupe, Renard writes that East Indians came from various professions and backgrounds, but they were mainly from the inferior castes.[23] These figures are misleading essentially for two reasons. First, the colonial authorities were lax at recordkeeping, and, second, Indians used this loophole and gave false information about themselves in order to gain new status in the Caribbean. Manipulating one's identity was not always successful or encouraging, however. Those who were discovered were ridiculed and even beaten by members of their community, which must have discouraged emigrants from falsifying their caste.[24] It would have been difficult and demanding for East Indians to "up-caste" themselves to falsify their caste identity without being discovered. Additionally, there would have been little incentive for East Indians to up-caste themselves since many came with the intention of going back to their respective localities in India. Nonetheless, it was possible that some East Indians did so up-caste themselves upon arrival in the Caribbean, especially in the case of those who assumed the surname "Maharaj", which was not a caste name in India but rather the title of a ruler.

The Breakdown of the Caste System on the Plantations

The fundamental principles of caste began to break down while East Indians were in transit to the Caribbean. Keith Laurence believes that because all castes were placed in a limited space on board the ships to the Caribbean, it was quite impossible to maintain caste purity, especially in area of dining.[25] Nothing more humorously explains the beginning of the disappearance of the caste system in Indian overseas communities than an old Indian woman's experience on board a ship bound for a sugar plantation in Fiji. She said each caste had its own cooking fireside, then a wave rocked the ship and all different foods were mixed. It was a choice of eating the mixed, polluted food or going hungry.[26] The mere act of leaving India meant the loss of caste, and to East Indians in India all those in the Caribbean were outcaste. But caste status could be reclaimed through a purification ceremony in India and could be bought in the Caribbean colonies. O'Malley claims that Gandhi, after his first visit to England, was excommunicated by the leaders of his caste community in Bombay and Porbandar, whereas the members of his caste at his home in Rajkot received him back into the communion.[27] By contrast, Bronkhurst informs us that a Hindu labourer belonging to the Vellalan caste nearly lost everything he had for eating in a Pariah-man's house in Trinidad, but money helped him to regain his caste status.[28] As in rural communities in colonial India, justice in indentured Caribbean East Indian communities sometimes revolved around customs rather than the law. Whenever East Indian customs and Western laws clashed, the latter usually prevailed, however. Thus, in the European Caribbean colonies an individual could have reclaimed in a court of law whatever he might have lost with regard to breaking any caste rules.

The caste system gave way quickly where the Caribbean East Indian population was relatively small (in Grenada, St Lucia and St Vincent, for example). Their small numbers coupled with opportunities for social and economic advancement made the process of cultural assimilation inevitable. Western plantation work routine, missionaries' efforts, Western influence, including the exposure to Western languages and shortages of women, caused the breakdown of the caste system in these communities. Caste does not exist in the Caribbean where the East Indian population is relatively small.

The caste system also went through a major transformation in territories where East Indians became a majority of the population (Guyana, Trinidad and Suriname). Comins reports that, in Trinidad, caste was not important among indentured servants and many caste prejudices were either modified or maticated.[29] Children of East Indian indentured servants in the colony of British Guiana were quite different from their parents, to the extent that it was difficult to conceive they were from the same family. The reason for this transformation was the freedom from the narrowness of caste prejudice.[30] Nearly all subsequent studies confirmed that caste did not exist, evoke or play important functions in East Indian overseas communities, except in Uganda, where, in the late nineteenth century, East Indians were brought to build a railway station from Mombasa to Lake Victoria Nyanza.

Morris observes that, though East Indians in Uganda were not successful in transferring the caste system, they were able to maintain a *jati* (sub-caste) identity.[31] This was possible because they maintained links with India and reinforced homeland ties of caste exclusiveness, which became "one of the most important structural principles in organizing Indian social life in East Africa".[32] The application of caste exclusiveness was not the same as in India. As such, the practice of homeland links with other overseas East Indian communities was not so strong and, consequently, contributed to the breakdown of the caste system there.

The conventional East Indian caste system disappeared in the Caribbean for various reasons. The most fundamental reasons were localized caste characteristics along with the capricious nature of the Caribbean plantation complex. It was a cultural clash between two different worlds in which the powerful plantation work routine prevailed. The East Indian occupational caste system operated along rank, duty, purity and so on. By contrast, the Caribbean sugar planters did not facilitate or fertilize caste rules. The sugar planters crushed discordant and disagreeable elements against them and promoted rivalry amongst various groups. To prevent or disrupt unity, they encouraged fissiparous tendencies, organized and grouped quisling castes and chose indentured servants who spoke three or four different languages. This deliberate mixing of emigrants and the policy of balance and counterpoise strengthened the security of the planter class and made it impossible for East Indians to transplant the caste system successfully in the Caribbean. The diversity among the emigrants also stymied any single standard of behaviour in the new environment. Even if East Indians had come from the same background, it would have been difficult for them to exercise the caste status system known in India – domination and restriction – partly because of the inflexible nature of the plantation system and partly because economic opportunities, although limited, opened possibilities for upward social mobility to East Indians of all castes after they finished their terms of contract. Consequently, the caste system broke down, as pointed out by one indentured servant in Trinidad:

all e de Indian	all of the Indians
all e come from Calcutta	all came from Calcutta
some different	some were different

some dhome (weaver) have	some were weavers
some kattik (teacher) have	some were religious teachers
chamar (low caste)	some were from the low caste
same wuk e doing	doing the same work
i wukking	working
brahan	Brahman
chatri (warrior caste) orking	kshatriya
all a dem orking	all of them working
you coming ork hyar	everyone came to work
you ha to ork	you have to work
same cutlass	with the same cutlass
same kudari (hoe)	with the same hoe
same hoe same man going hauling cutlass	with the same working tools
if a chatri	if you are a kshatriya
if a Brahman	if you are a Brahman
if a naw (barber)	if you are a barber
if a dhome (weaver)	if you are a weaver
if a kattik (teacher)	if you are a teacher
ha to come to ork.[33]	you have to work on the plantations
	(author's translation)

As pointed out above, all castes worked on the sugar plantations doing a variety of menial jobs. The caste system subsequently broke down and assumed a new, reversed status. Indeed, East Indians entered another form of caste in which they were stratified according to the expectations of the planters. To the planters, it became increasingly clear that the low castes were the best workers, the middle castes good workers and the upper castes the worst workers.[34] The upper castes refused to work and on occasions invoked disturbances on the plantations. To appease them, the planters offered them light work and even allowed them to refrain from work altogether. Bechu, a Bengali Christian, was given a high-caste status by the colonial administration for his "radicalism". Bechu stunned colonial authorities with his eloquence when he spoke and fought on behalf of indentured East Indians against the system.[35] The colonial authorities also believed Oederman, a Brahman, was one of the ringleaders of the Devonshire Caste Disturbance of 1872 in British Guiana.[36] Upper-caste indentured servants were also proud of their cultural heritage and were a major obstacle to evangelical colonialism; that is, the conversion of East Indian indentured servants to Christianity. During the nineteenth and early twentieth centuries in Trinidad, Canadian Christian catechist, John Morton, stated that he did not understand what pride was until he met a member of the upper caste.[37] Their influence was so strong in creating disturbances and riots on the sugar estates and preventing other indentured East Indians from joining Christianity that the colonial administration tried to stop their entry into the Caribbean.[38] The planters favoured low-caste over high-caste East Indians partly for security reasons and partly because low-caste workers were more dedicated.

In an environment where conditions and thought patterns of life were changing and memories and identities were being re-evaluated and reconstructed one would expect the dissonant and dissident low-caste East Indians to be diametrically opposed to the consecrative and ceremonial caste ideologies of patriotism. Indeed, there was the development of a subculture within a subculture in which the semi-free play of polarities and pluralities repeatedly characterized indentured communities. Low-caste servants grabbed the slightest opportunity, though within certain limitations, to abandon the traditional caste system and adapt semi-Western ways. Other servants chose to identify with the cultural folkways, mores and values of other ethnic groups such as the Amerindians, Africans, Portuguese, Chinese and Javanese. East Indians had long noticed Western behaviour among their fellow Indians in India, but were unable to emulate these behavioural styles because of caste restrictions. East Indians were also familiar with *Arya Samaj* (Association of the Respected Ones), a North Indian reformist sect founded in Bombay in 1875, known for, *inter alia*, its anti-caste doctrines and the rejection of Brahman supremacy. The teaching of *Arya Samaj* exposed Indians to a differentiated vision of life, one that essentially allowed them the liberty to re-examine and re-evaluate their religious beliefs. The Brahmans and other high castes, however, counteracted *Arya Samaj* and consolidated their beliefs into one single tradition, *Sanatan Dharma* (Eternal Religion).[39] This behaviour was noticed soon after the collapse of the indenture system in 1920.

In the Caribbean, the plantation system successfully suppressed the caste prescriptions and proscriptions of indentured servants. This provided the opportunity for low-caste indentured servants to disregard restrictive caste rules. The relaxation of the caste rules on the plantations allowed low-caste indentured servants for the first time to experience a sense of worth, if not a rebirth. They took conscious, deliberate steps to bolster a renewed sense of identity, from being mindless and gullible to industrious. For this reason the retention of some aspects of the caste system was found more in East Indian communities (reinforced by new immigrants) and less so on the plantations.

The Breakdown of the Caste System in Indentured Communities

The caste system also broke down in East Indian indentured communities. Although the plantation system isolated Indian communities from other ethnic groups, it was not concerned with how these communities lived but how they functioned on the plantations. Indentured servants were housed in "nigger yards" throughout the indenture period. Nigger yards – also called *Camp des Noirs* in French territories – were the abandoned living quarters of freed African slaves. The living conditions of indentured servants were quite similar to those of slaves. For instance, one barrack housed about two hundred indentured people.[40] These living quarters were neglected, but more importantly, only few officials understood the importance of caste to indentured servants. Communities, therefore, had to rely on their culture and customs – which had embedded caste characteristics – to cope and cohere. As they turned to their ancestral culture for reassurance, however, they realized that this was not entirely possible because of the rise in socioeconomic status of low-caste indentured servants, particularly on the plantations. These low-caste servants were not willing to perpetuate the restrictive caste system in the Caribbean, and so the social structure of indentured communities began to change from within. Indentured servants began to assimilate into the Caribbean class system. This transition from caste to class in indentured East Indian communities meant that indentured servants adjusted to new Western forms and interpretations of race, class and gender relationships, further disintegrating the importance of caste cohesion. This social transformation also widened the gap between East Indians from India and Caribbean

East Indians, from East Indians on the plantations (at work) and from East Indians in the communities (at home).

The transition and transcendence from caste to class was not a somniferous and soothing passage. In particular, the People's Association of British Guiana and the Trinidad Working Men's Association (mainly black middle class) spoke openly against the further immigration of indentured East Indians to British Guiana and Trinidad. For this, and other reasons, East Indian indentured servants turned to Western-educated East Indians to confront, deal with and represent them in issues that affected their general welfare. They were particularly concerned about the legalization of East Indian marriages performed according to traditional rites, shelters for the destitute, free return passage rights and the general right to be treated fairly by the larger Caribbean society. Many secular organizations, such as the East Indian National Association in Couva and the East Indian National Congress in Princes Town in Trinidad, the British Guiana East Indian Association, and the Suriname Immigrants' Association, began to emerge in the last decade of the indentureship. Leaders of these organizations (Jules Mahabir, Metha Jaimini [1928] in Trinidad, Joseph and Peter Ruhoman in British Guiana, and Sital Persaud and Lutchman Singh in Suriname, for example) helped East Indian communities deal with the transition from caste to class and other challenging socioeconomic factors like the lack of education and representation in an increasingly creolized Caribbean class society. Yet, the emergence of an East Indian middle class did not mean that this class was all pro-East Indian. Some lived separate social lives. They were still attached to the East Indian communities through their occupations, but were caught in the quagmire of traditional and Western customs. For the majority, particularly the traditional and partially westernized East Indians, their world did not really extend beyond the Immigration Department. Their mere existence revolved around a narrow and limited sphere of thought and action, and they therefore were unable to adapt to the changing conditions successfully. Many came to rely on their own inner resources of survival and communal wisdom to guide their daily actions. It was not surprising then that the East Indian indentured communities continued to turn to the high caste (Brahmans), the village headmen (*Patwari*), the drivers and even the shopkeepers for guidance and inspiration and to perform important cultural functions as they had done in India. Nowhere was this more emphasized than in a folk song of indentured servants:

> I bow to that Brahman, who reads me the *Katha*
> Who teaches me the *puja, sandhya* and *havan*.
> And
> Hail to the Brahmans who built the temple here,
> who save us from the exploitation of the missions.[41]

The caste system in indentured communities was not entirely transformed into a class system. Rather, two extreme forms – the Brahman and the Chamar or the "high nation" and the "low nation" – emerged. The other castes in between vanished. The Brahmans remained leaders and the Chamars remained followers of indentured East Indian communities. East Indian communities, therefore, became socially stratified in relation to the Brahman beliefs and values. The Brahmans reasserted their monopoly over important ritualistic functions, which were needed by East Indian communities to meet the demands of birth, marriage and death.[42] Their status was recognized mainly in East Indian quarters and less so on the plantations since the latter disregarded their religious importance. Nonetheless, their presence in the Caribbean was extremely important in providing East Indians psychological protection against racial and cultural hostility.[43] The Brahmans were perceived by indentured East Indian communities to be the carriers, interpreters and transmitters of Hinduism within the Caribbean.

In the latter stages of the indenture system, however, the importance of the "high nation" or Brahmans began to decline. Apart from priesthood, many had various occupations such as farmers, rum shop proprietors and truck drivers which were at variance with their homeland culture, but did not contradict the concept of purity in Hinduism. The indenture system, by its very limited nature, understandably did not produce a galaxy of brilliant Caribbean Brahmans and, subsequently, many were no longer well-versed in reading and discussing the scriptures of Hinduism. (This author, through ethnographic research, noticed fascinating as well as fallacious arguments among older generation Caribbean Hindus about who could read or write

Sanskrit thoroughly. Most of these arguments generally took place at the "wake house" or in any informal meeting place. On some occasions, they were just instigated by younger East Indians for the sake of providing humour.) The limited knowledge of the Brahman pandits or priests, obtained through memorization of songs, poems and verses as well as their ability to discuss Hinduism, however deficient, was accepted by the wider indentured community. During the indentured period, and apparent in Caribbean society today, after work, or on religious occasions, East Indians gathered in small groups to chant various epics from the Hindu scriptures. Hinduism in the Caribbean has evolved into an elastic and antinomic religion, incorporating and synchronizing various strands from animal sacrifice to intense spiritual discourses. These strands were historically replenished by the arrival of fresh indentured servants and occasional visits by well-versed pandits from India.

This elastic or liberal view of Hinduism was the catalyst for allowing some of the "low-nation" indentured servants to gain entry into the once-restricted Brahman priesthood through exposure to Western education and socioeconomic achievements on the sugar plantations. These developments blurred caste distinctions between "low nation" and the "high nation" in indentured communities. Servants began to realize that prominent positions in indentured Caribbean communities could be achieved without ascribed status or rank. As a result, internal social stratification decreased and status differentiation based on education, economic power and profession became important. Specifically, endogamy and the Brahman's right through birth to special roles diminished. Even the privilege of being considered "twice-born" (a concept referring to a ceremony at puberty whereby young men were initiated into adulthood and then into East Indian society) and the right to wear the "sacred thread" were not practised, prioritized or even recognized in the Caribbean. Furthermore, "low-nation" East Indians began to realize that the concept of dark skin being inferior in the caste system was at direct variance with the achievements made by Afro-Caribbeans not only on the plantations (overseers, headmen, supervisors) but in the field of education (headmasters, teachers, lawyers, labour union leaders).

Even though the caste system became a thing of the past in the latter stages of the indenture period, caste prejudice was not eliminated. Disputes and disagreements among indentured servants were treated along caste lines. Brahmans often resorted to caste status, informing and reminding low-caste servants of their low ancestral status. One common denigrating remark was that "a chamar is a chamar". This, however, was symbolic and had no implication, restriction or signification on socioeconomic mobility. On other occasions, name calling in regard to the caste system was an attempt to celebrate the historicist memory and to provide humour.

By the end of the indenture system, the caste system dissolved and the class system emerged in indentured Caribbean East Indian communities. These communities were also stratified according to power, privilege and prestige and along a three-tiered system with a small elite at the top, a larger low class at the bottom and a middle class in between. Indentured communities were then different from the wider Caribbean society in language, culture and custom, but were similar in social and economic structure.

Joint Family System and Cultural Continuity

The East Indian joint family system in India has been placed in a series of compositional categories: collateral joint family, supplemented collateral joint family, supplemented lineal joint family, lineal-collateral joint family and supplemented lineal-collateral joint family.[44] Despite these differences, the Indian joint family includes a man and wife, their married daughters, sons and spouses, and the children of sons.[45] Daughters are expected to leave their families and reside with their husbands' families. Authority within the joint family is determined by sex and age. The eldest man maintains authority over the family while older members have control over younger members of the family. This family group is characteristically patrilineal in descent, patrilocal in residence and patriarchal in authority. Property inheritance is equally shared among adult men lineally related for at least four generations. The East Indian joint family is more than just a matter concerning household size, common living space, sharing of property, incomes, chores and so on. Milton Singer offers an interesting explanation of a typical Indian joint family:

As a social structure, a joint family is a network of social relations among persons related in specified ways. These social relations are crystallized in a set of mutual obligations within a framework of law or customary usages which defines appropriate norms of behaviour for each category of relative. Whether a particular group of persons constitutes a joint family depends on whether this group of persons is held together by the kind of social network in question, that is, whether the individuals within it are disposed to discharge towards one another the set of rights and duties specified in their religious scriptures, legal code and customary usages. The presence of any particular feature does not necessarily make a group of people a joint family, nor its absence deprive the group of that status.[46]

Most Indian families do not differentiate between joint and nuclear families and regard any sort of family as a natural outgrowth of the original family. Joint family patterns, in terms of rights and duties, in India have received a great deal of attention.[47] Most studies have highlighted the strengths and securities of central decision-making, income pooling and supporting kinship. These filial–fraternal networks have helped Indian families survive and have brought a "peace of mind" to their individual members.

Despite the advantages of the joint family, cohesion and cooperation have not always been served and maintained. Internal quarrels between mothers-in-law and wives, between fathers and sons, and among brothers have caused families to split into smaller households. More often the split is repaired and family ties are restored and resumed, even though relatives may continue to live in different households. Parallel to this reconciliation, however, is that partition among families has taken place in bitterness, where family members do not speak to each other. The father's curse over a departed son is still feared in India, and sons who break joint family relationships are seen as a disgrace, unless there is some plausible excuse to leave.[48] Disputes, however, are common among families world over. Conflict theorist Karl Marx believed that it is within family that abuse and conflict are more profound particularly in gender relations. Women tend to have few avenues for self-expression and personal development.

The East Indian joint family system was not transferred to the Caribbean where indentured servants were a majority, until the 1870s when they were given land to settle in lieu of return passage to India. A number of factors

4. A descendant of East Indian indentured servants cutting sugar cane. Conditions are somwhat similar to those in the days of indentured servitude.

prevented the transferral of this system to the Caribbean before the 1870s. First, most emigrants did not come with their families. Instead, they came as single contract workers, each signing his or her contract. Furthermore, the differences among emigrants according to race, religion and language were too profound to forge any meaningful common ground in the early phase of indenture service. Second, the emigration agents favoured a predominantly male labour force, recruiting fewer women than men. Not only did the sex disparity undermine family life, but it also created social and moral problems on the estates. East Indian men competed for scarce East Indian women, and this led to jealousy and wife murders. Third, some families which were recruited to labour in the Caribbean were not the typical joint family of India. Since there were many loopholes in the emigration process, women and men desperately conjured up family relations in order to embark. The colonial authorities were pressured to support family life on the Caribbean plantations and paid little attention to the important characteristics of the East Indian joint family system. They were busy trying to meet the basic requirements and quota. The depot family relations were broken up by the plantation system and the East Indians themselves when these families reached the Caribbean. Many never saw each other again. Fourth, despite the paucity of women and other social handicaps, East Indians, particularly in Guyana and Trinidad, stuck to themselves, and only a few joined with other ethnic groups. Fifth, in the first decades of the indenture system (1838–1870), the colonial authorities recycled indentured servants from India to the Caribbean and back. This practice discouraged the re-formation of the joint family system.

The nature of the plantation system also affected the stability of East Indian family life in the Caribbean. East Indian contract workers suffered somewhat the same degree of inhumanity that characterized the Africans' experience in the Caribbean during the slave period. On arrival, East Indians were partitioned and sent to various plantations. They were housed in barracks and *logies* (abandoned slave quarters) and worked long hours under extreme conditions. The principal difference between slavery and indenture was that the former had no contracted end in sight, while the latter had a termination time, at which time East Indians were allowed to return home or to acquire a piece of land. These

5. *Getting ready to load the sugar cane into punts. The oxen are used to pull the punts to and from the fields by the way of canals.*

6. Loading the sugar cane into punts. The sugar cane is carried manually on the head of the cane cutter, who would have to make at least two hundred trips to fill the punt.

circumstances, combined with the planter's lack of interest in providing a home life for indentured workers, undermined the re-establishment of the East Indian joint family in the Caribbean. Then, how were they able to re-construct some aspects of the joint family during the latter part of the indenture system?

The indenture system was not incommensurably bad or evil. Its combination of semi-free and free labour distinguished it from previous forms of unfree labour in the Caribbean. Indeed, it was even different from other indentured labour systems in the Americas. It was regulated and supervised by the state which, if not necessarily in the spirit of liberal-humanitarian sentiments, provided a few incentives. The colonial administration offered East Indians parcels of land to settle in the Caribbean mainly to ease the burden of paying the return passages. As the East Indian population was reaching substantial numbers, communities were clustering around the sugar plantations. East Indians themselves began to view the Caribbean as home, where certain expectations of livelihood could be realized. Many accepted small parcels of land and, with their accumulation of wealth, collectively and individually, were able to make the transition from plantation exploitation to community life. By the 1870s, land commutation and land acquisition were the catalyst for a marked division and difference in East Indian indentured communities: some were independent peasant proprietors and self-employed, while others were attached to the plantations on a part-time basis. Yet, many were still tied to the plantation system and availed themselves of basic incentives (free housing, free health care, steady wages) of the plantation system. Whatever might have been the status of East Indians, certain dominant trends began to appear or reappear. One trend was the remarkable re-establishment of their homeland culture, bordering on a sort of a cultural renaissance. This re-establishment actually began in the depot and as indentured servants were in transit to the Caribbean. From various backgrounds, they developed relationships and social ties of *Jahaji Bhai* and *Bahin* (ship-brother and ship-sister) to console, cohere and co-exist. Over and beyond this, there was an attempt to identify common bonds – culture and traditions – that would hold them together. Although these bonds were jarred on the authoritative controlled sugar estates,[49] they were nonetheless the basis for preserving and securing traditions at the grassroots level as well as accommodating and sustaining diversity among the emigrants. They also provided the bases for the relocation and resuscitation of the East Indian joint family system in the Caribbean.

By the last decades of the indenture system, the colonial administration did not entirely determine or dictate what was best for indentured communities in terms of socialization and education. This policy inadvertently led to the restoration of East Indian joint family life in the Caribbean. Indentured servants expressed their love for rural life and joint family relationships. Community kinship ties among indentured servants were based on fictive relations that included immediate neighbours and friends of families.[50] Of particular importance in these communities was the maintenance of the joint family (for example, pooling of resources, functions of work duties and obligations, male authority and so on) and the willingness to put aside certain ingrained differences (for example, the Muslim and Hindu differences and the concept of pure versus impure in the caste system). Moreover, their ability to stick together emerged from the negative attitude they encountered or received from European and Creole ways, the overall unpredictable external powers and pressures of the plantation system and an appreciation for their homeland culture.

The East Indian joint family system during the indenture period bore an interesting resemblance to its model in India. The father–son relationship was based on respect and was taught early in life. The son had to be obedient in front of his parents even under the firmest of parental control. He was expected to behave circumspectly in the presence of his father. Open discussions, loud laughing, sitting on higher stools, smoking and drinking were unwelcome behaviours. Fathers generally held great affection for their sons but rarely expressed it openly. They wielded enormous authority over their sons and family until they were quite old. A son's dependence on his father was sanctioned and sanctified in Hindu scriptures.[51]

Like similar familial systems in the world, the East Indian joint family experienced many personal strains. In India, when a son leaves his family, voluntarily or by force, Hindu family law rules that he is entitled to his ascribed share of the property. But most East Indians think it is desirable for married sons to live, work and share the property with their parents and to remain together until death.[52] Family customs generally supersede the law. There are also predictable strains between the mother-in-law and daughter-in-law. Through arranged marriages, young wives are sometimes strangers in their new homes. Daughter-in-law and mother-in-law often have opposite interests in an East Indian joint family system. The daughter-in-law is interested in strengthening the bonds with her husband and children, while the mother-in-law is interested in the welfare of the extended household.[53] In the eyes of the mother-in-law, the daughter-in-law's every action is to be criticized to keep her in "line".

Under the indenture system, and even in the contemporary period, these differences were irreconcilable, often leading to the daughter-in-law to suicide. One folk song in Suriname testified to such an action:

My mother-in-law gave (me) a full kilo of wheat.
Daughter-in-law, come on (won't you?) (to) grind (the wheat into) flour.
After grinding when I bring the flour (I say):
Mother-in-law, weigh up (won't you?) your flour.
The mother-in-law places the kilo (weight) and the nanad two kilos
(And) the lord himself places a complete kilo.
The mother-in-law pushes upwards, the nanad pushes downwards.
The lord himself gives (a hit with a) sword.
In this very mood of disenchantment the precious one took up (her) pitcher;

(And) (She) went to (fetch) water (from the) lake or the pond
Having filled the pitchers (she) placed (them) on the platform
(She) took off her clothes and took a dip, bathing.
(she) took one dip, took the second dip
In the third (dip) she drowned (herself) in the pond.[54]

Although these tensions were found in the joint family of indentured servants, they were more an exception than the norm. Some authoritative patterns were challenged because there were no official penalties for non-compliance to traditional norms in the Caribbean. Conformity to tradition was perpetuated by personal commitment and varied among social class and families, such as fathers' authority over sons and mothers' control over their sons' wives. Inter-familial relationships were not guided by scriptures or by customs, but by economic and social forces. The most educated members were accorded the most respect, especially in smaller joint family systems. Seniority played a less important role.

By the end of the indenture system, the East Indian joint family system started to change. Although the general living arrangements were extended, a semi-nuclear family system emerged, composed of a man, a woman and unmarried children. The nuclear household was often an attachment to the original household or was built separately in the same plot of land. Members interacted like a joint family, but at the end of the day everyone retreated to his or her own household. Young couples continued to live with their maternal or parental parents for a few months or a few years until they became economically independent enough to move "one side". Smith and Jayawardena found in British Guiana soon after the indenture period that

When the young couples marry it is customary for them to go to live at the home of the bridegroom's parents, the bride becoming a member of that household group. They are normally dependent upon the head of the household for food and clothing and contribute anything they earn to the common purse. The wife does household chores under the direction of her mother-in-law, but gradually the couple begins to assert their independence. A new hearth is built in the kitchen for the young wife and then she begins to keep a separate larder, perhaps continuing to share some of the cooking utensils. Eventually the couple breaks away and sets up their own household in a separate building.[55]

There was often pressure on the couple from the parents, in-laws and the community at large to move into their own place. Often parents and other family members criticized couples openly for "playing the fool" or "skinning their teeth" for lagging behind in finding their own place.

From the 1870s to 1920 and as in so many other communities in the Caribbean during the nineteenth century, East Indian indentured servants had to reinvent their environment and their joint family through myth, memory, mind or manner. This reinvention and reconstruction faced myriad challenges. Indentured servants had to deal with arduous daily work routines on the plantation, which offered material rather than cultural benefits. The parcelling of small plots of land by the colonial government to individual indentured servants was an important factor in the re-formation of the joint family system. Land ownership provided them the opportunity to move away from a life entirely controlled by the plantation. They were able to engage in other activities consonant with rural life and large supporting families, such as rice and cocoa farming. The interplay between sugar and rice cultivation, the former on a full-time basis and latter on a seasonal basis, led to economic security and the formulation of strong cultural ties among indentured servants. At the centre of this process was the joint family, which provided a deep anchorage in terms of survival and pride. Large supporting families became a necessity during the latter stages of the indenture period. Indentured servants began to feel comfortable with rural life and developed what sociologists call *Gemeinschaft* bonds/communities or mechanical solidarity (shared values and identities with one another and moral consensus). This was instrumental in dealing with anomie. Shared values were necessary, not nostalgic sentiments. In these communities, there was a sense of rediscovering local autonomy and resuscitating local pride as their ancestors would have known in India. Large families were seen as God's blessing. These characteristics reflected the values of these communities.

Another reason for the maintenance of the joint family was to ensure the successful transition from dependence on the indenture system to independent survival. In the absence of sound developmental strategies with regard to guaranteed social security or medical and employment insurance and in a system where there was the reluctance to take up the "white man's burden", indentured servants created coping mechanisms for themselves by themselves. The continuation of large joint families was one such mechanism, for it served as an economic asset and a motif of survival. Families stayed together and relied on each individual member, young and old, for support. It was a kind of insurance for all, especially the physically or mentally deficient. Thus, by the end of the indentured period, two social organizations and social families surfaced that were semi-opposed to each other. One revealed the shift towards individualism and the other clung to the old East Indian conception of the group or the joint family as the basic organizational unit. These attitudes were determined by the socioeconomic standing of indentured servants.

It is interesting to note that, unlike Europe where there was at this time a movement to embrace nuclear family settings under the axiom and hermeneutic of social progress, Caribbean East Indians were synthesizing and synchronizing the individual as well as the group concepts of family. There were many reasons for this, but the most fundamental is expressed in the six systems of Indian philosophy (*Nyaya, Vaishesika, Samkya, Yoga, Mimamsa* and *Vedenta*). These encourage individualistic principles and inner perfection, but emphasize that social structure should revolve around communal and group ideals.[56] Notwithstanding, the East Indian family was not free of social problems. They experienced cognitive dissonance where their beliefs did not match or complement their actions. This was not at all surprising, especially since the centre of gravity stood outside of their control. Contemporary East Indian Caribbean communities still face the challenges of effective social integration and efficient economic development. Many are lost in the labyrinth of daily struggles. Imagine how much harder it must have been for indentured East Indians to have maintained a social structure in a land of new varieties. Confusion and contradiction were ineluctable consequences of indentured experience. But they survived such consternation by relying on the joint family. Central to the survival of the joint family was the role of women, to whom we turn in the next chapter.

Chapter 4

Indo-Caribbean Women: Daughters of Sacrifice and Survival

Women's Roles in India

The previous chapter demonstrated how the shedding of obsolete cultural beliefs and the retention of cultural practices helped indentured servants adapt to the regimen of plantation life. This chapter extends the argument that indentured servants were not entirely suppressed by the indenture system. Indo-Caribbean women used the Third Space between European imperialist patriarchy, at the top, and East Indian patriarchy, at the bottom, as a place of agency to articulate and maintain their cultural identity.

The historical attitude of East Indian women prior to their arrival to the Caribbean was complex and multi-faceted, ranging from defeatism to determination and from resignation to resurgence. Perhaps it is best to begin with the negative aspects, for no apparent argumentative reasons, but to show how the lives of East Indian women might have improved over the years. Women in India have always experienced fewer privileges than men. In early India, women suffered from the indignities of an uncivilized society as it was making the transition from barbarism to civilization. Women were persecuted and abandoned for the slightest infraction and were even sold and resold. They were slaves and were seen as inferior to men in both skill and strength. Apart from daily abuses, women were also stripped of basic rights and privileges. The East Indian patriarchal system reduced them to the lowest status in society. They lived and accepted their inevitable position. Some scholars note that, on the whole, the status of East Indian women has deteriorated for the last two thousand years.[1] Among the reasons for this decline have been the lack of educational opportunities, child marriage, widowhood, *sati*, patriarchy, preference for sons and the Laws of Manu. The last is essentially a theoretical treatise on the social order of Hinduism from the point of view of the Brahmans. It was allegedly prescribed by India's mythical founding ruler, Manu, in the first or second century BC. One section of the Laws of Manu states that women are incapable of taking care of themselves, and therefore they have to depend on the male gender to survive: their father before marriage, their husband after marriage and their son when their husband is no more.[2]

The practice of *sati* deserves a brief discussion. *Sati* is a practice whereby wives joined the funeral pyre of their husbands and burned with the dead body. The earliest evidence of *sati* in India was in AD 510, and was more common among the upper kshatriya caste. The practice was probably brought to India originally by the Scytho-Tartars, among whom the custom prevailed of vassals and liegemen killing themselves on the death of their lord.[3] In Indian society, the death of a husband plunged the widow automatically into a marginal position. All her attachments with her husband before his death, except for property rights, ceased to exist. However, this was more in theory than in practice, since East Indian customs dictated that a widow's wealth belonged to her son. Being ostracized by her husband's family and considered worthless by her community, she generally found it difficult to lead an enforced celibate life and live up to the principles of Hinduism.

Sati was voluntary and compulsory. Some widows approached the pyre with great heroism, and all castes often applauded their meritorious behaviour. If widows failed to live up to their courage and take the pyre voluntarily, they were drugged so that they would not escape the inevitable. Countless stories told of women who collapsed before reaching the fearful altar or fled the pyre only to be captured and brought back. Raja Budh Singh of Bundi took eighty-four *satis* with him, and Ajit Singh of Jodhpur took sixty-four. However, twenty was the most common number among the high caste.

The Raja of Idar took seven queens, two concubines, four female slaves and one personal manservant to the pyre. In 1807, three hundred *satis* were recorded within a ten-mile radius of Calcutta.⁴ The principal reasons that widows ascended funeral pyres was, first, to ensure they would not bring disgrace to the deceased husband's family by committing some improper act and, second, to deny them their share of the family's property.

Despite the aforementioned indications of female subjection to the male, there were numerous indications that women often played an important role in East Indian society. Particularly, the Hindu codes of behaviour stressed that women should be treated with respect. The *Shakti* cult, for example, emphasized the equality between men and women as well as the power of women.⁵ East Indians appeared to be fascinated by female sexuality, and tradition held that women often used their sexual powers to achieve dominance over men. The respect and sexuality of women are expressed in the main epics of Hinduism. The principles of male and female togetherness in the great epics of the *Mahabharata, Ramayana* and *Kama Sutra* provided divinity, hope and inspiration for East Indian women. They also enjoyed a degree of freedom in religious asceticism, by providing the opportunity for women to escape the perils of condemnation, discrimination and exploitation. Female ascetics generally followed one of two types of lifestyle: an active life, moving between pilgrimage centres begging for survival, and a stationary life, living contemplatively at a monastery. Female monastic ascetics followed strict rules, while independent female ascetics enjoyed a considerable degree of freedom, especially when compared to other East Indian women.⁶ Most Hindus contend that women should lead a religious life within their society, preferably within the household.

The position of women began to change markedly when the British entered India. Although the imposition of British despotic rule in India undoubtedly had a negative effect, it nonetheless raised the position of East Indian women and brought changes to traditional, patriarchal India. British imperialistic aims, economic and otherwise, interfered with East Indian customs, dismantling some rigid social structures for the reason that European ways were morally superior. This attitude devastated the moral fabric of East Indian society and certainly added to the swelling of the lower caste in India. Nevertheless, British policies also inadvertently eroded some undesirable accretions of Hinduism and Islam. As far as gender was concerned, they were guided by a simple formula: "Among rude people, the women are generally degraded; among civilized people they are exalted."[7] This liberal view of women was used to construct and validate Western superiority, casting odium on indigenous customs. Towards that end, British colonial objectives and East Indian conventional thinking of women came into direct conflict.

The British were stunned by the extreme degradation women suffered in India. In unison with East Indian social reformers such as Ishwar Chandra, Vidyasager and Swami Dayananda (through Arya Samaj) and Rajaram Mohan Roy (through Brahmo Samaj), they sought to transform attitudes. By the mid-nineteenth century, reform groups resonated throughout India. The liberal views they introduced, which advocated greater freedom for women, gained ubiquitous currency in India. The social reformers focused mainly on reforming the customs of *sati*, child marriage, female infanticide, *purdah*, female education, Indian joint family relationships and the *devadisis* (Hindu women temple dancers).[8] The result was that "between 1772 and 1947, the British introduced nine major laws liberalizing women's legal position in British India, including those forbidding female infanticide, sati and child marriage and those raising the age of consent, allowing widow remarriage and improving women's inheritance rights".[9] The work of the reformers was instrumental in bringing social change to India, outlawing certain abuses and restrictions on women. After centuries of marginalization, East Indian women found opportunities for self-expression and their status improved. There were areas where reforms were less progressive, since old attitudes of prejudice against women in East Indian society were still persistent, however. Nevertheless, the position of women in India improved markedly considering that for a long time they had been placed in positions of great disadvantage and outside the realms of self-expression.

This brief historical and social analysis of Hindu women in India before they emigrated to the Caribbean in the nineteenth century suggests that they were beginning to experience greater freedom. They were granted some commiseration and enjoyed a certain amount of control over their individuality. How much the Caribbean plantation system would emancipate East Indian women or excoriate them of their freedom will be one of the central themes addressed in the following sections.

Sex Disparity among Indian Emigrants Under Indenture

The post-emancipation immigration scheme of indentured servants was marked by a noticeable shortage of women. The recruitment and emigration of women were governed by a quota system imposed by the Colonial Office and the Government of India. When the indenture system started in British Guiana in 1838, for instance, the female–male ratio of East Indian emigrants was 3:100. Serious social problems arising from this kind of disparity led the colonial authorities to establish quotas for women migrating to the West Indian colonies. By 1870, the ratio of forty women to one hundred men was fixed and was required before any shipment of East Indians could commence. Very rarely was this quota met, and it never exceeded the stipulated number of women needed for Caribbean sugar colonies. Only 25 per cent of East Indian emigrants who boarded ships for the West Indies were women.[10] Table 4 shows the proportion of females introduced to St Lucia from 1859 to 1891.

Table 4: Number of East Indians Introduced to St Lucia, 1859–1891

Ships	Year	Male	Female
Palmyra	1859	244	69
Francis Ridley	1859	169	83
Victor Emmanuel	1860	312	74
Zemindar	1860	228	82
Ulysses	1862	250	64
Leonidas	1878	330	190
Chetah	1879	330	85
Foyle	1880	43	21
Bann	1881	224	88
Bracadaile	1884	350	134
Poonah	1885	167	81
Roumania	1891	319	134

Source: D.W.D. Comins, *Notes on Emigration from India to St Lucia* (Calcutta: Bengal Secretariat, 1893), 3–4.

Some scholars point to several reasons why there was a shortage of East Indian women in the West Indian colonies:

1. Caribbean planters saw women as a financial burden to the plantation system because of child rearing.
2. Caribbean planters preferred a predominantly male labour force because men were better suited for plantation work under harsh tropical conditions.
3. Women were reluctant to emigrate overseas because of restrictions placed on them and the negative attitudes of patriarchal society.
4. East Indian men did not want their young wives to travel with them.
5. Objections to the obligatory medical examination for women, which included examining genitals for various diseases.
6. Emigration agents were reluctant to recruit single women because it was believed that they would necessarily be from the low strata of society and therefore prostitutes (this class of women was believed to have been responsible for many social problems on the plantations, including wife murders).
7. Most recruitment took place in India where there was already a disparity of sexes.
8. East Indian caste, customs and culture discouraged women from emigrating.
9. Because so many regulations were attached to the recruitment of women, recruiters preferred male labourers.
10. Because there was a shortage of women available for or willing to emigrate in the first place, agents had to pay higher commissions to recruit women; this was a disincentive.[11]

Table 5 shows how much more recruiters were willing to pay for female East Indian emigrants.

Table 5: Amounts Paid by Recruiters for Emigrants (in Rupees)

No. of Emigrants	Rates for Men	Rates for Women
For 1 to 10	Rs. 35	Rs. 55
For 11 to 20	40	70
For 21 and over	45	80

Source: Public Record Office (Colonial Office), Note by Mr. C.W. Doorly on the Methods of Recruiting Emigrants in the Madras Presidency to Colonial Secretary, 30 October 1915, 571:30.

Certainly, these factors contributed to the paucity of East Indian women in the Caribbean under indenture.[12] Most importantly, fewer women than men emigrated because of the colonial administrative preferences and prejudices. The planters favoured a male labour force and reasoned that women would create more overhead costs – through childbearing and childcare – to an already ailing plantation system.[13] This argument was specious, since the evidence indicated that women under slavery were beneficial to the plantation system. Indeed, African women slaves worked on the plantations in large numbers, proved equally as productive as men and, more impressively, showed a higher survival rate than their male counterparts.[14] After slavery, nonetheless, planters were reluctant to have a sizable portion of women on the plantations, in spite of the fact that they were well aware that East Indian women were accustomed to hard agricultural work under blazing tropical heat in India. Women in India, especially rural women, performed many functions, from weaving, to childcare, to working in the fields and mines.[15] These were presumably the types of women the planters would have wanted in the Caribbean. So, the suggestion that planters favoured a male labour force because they did not want to accrue expenses is unlikely.

Throughout the indenture period, the planters complained loudly about how difficult it was to recruit East Indian women to emigrate. Colonial agents often claimed that "one of the greatest impediments to emigration from the East was the difficulty of procuring so large a percent of women" for the sugar colonies.[16] The emigration agent for British Guiana, Mitchell, wrote: "There can be little doubt the great majority of female emigrants are recruited literally from the streets whither they have been driven for the means of sustaining life either through the demise of their natural protectors or for domestic shortcomings."[17] However, these challenges alone cannot explain why the planters chose not to bring East Indian women to the Caribbean in equal numbers to men.

From the standpoint of the colonial administration, the implementation of the indenture system was a substitute for slavery on a temporary basis. Single men were regarded as the best possible solution to fulfil this labour requirement. They were easily secured when needed and usually returned home when the sugar industry was experiencing difficulties. The introduction of women on a large scale would have led to family relationships and a degree of permanency in the Caribbean, which would have undermined the planter's control of a predominantly male population. Moreover, family relationships would have encouraged an alternative vision of life among East Indian emigrants, one at variance with the indenture system. Taking into consideration the aseptic and authoritative structure of the indenture system, East Indians would have looked, as demonstrated throughout the period, for opportunities outside the confines of the plantations. Men were capable of making this transition, but the presence of women and families would have made this process less tenable. The colonial government granted East Indians small parcels of land to settle after 1870. This policy was not intended to promote family life, but rather to retain an immobile labour force which would be cheap for the sugar industry. Land settlement schemes were encouraged to avoid repatriation expenses and when the sugar industry faced a crisis, particularly during the depression in the 1880s through competition from European beet sugar.

Moreover, East Indian women emigrated with the principal aim of improving their social and economic position, even if this required severing ties with their homeland.[18] Their presence on the plantations was a direct threat to the planters' control because they were perceived collectively as a liberating force. The idea then that women would have been costly to the plantation system has not been borne out by the evidence.

East Indian women worked long hours in India, and on the Caribbean plantations they worked equally hard as men digging, planting, weeding and cutting sugar cane, even in the advanced stages of pregnancy. Some women even gave birth on the plantations. On his tour to the Caribbean, Comins found women in their last stages of pregnancy employed on sugar plantations in St Lucia.[19] Some of them sold provisions in the open markets on Saturdays. Others were saddled with the responsibilities of working and raising families, what contemporary feminists call the double burden. Married women were not obliged to work, and the indenture system dictated that the planters should provide them with rations, accommodations and medical care. Little was mentioned about single women whose relationships had not conformed to the legal definition of marriage.

East Indian marriages, whether they were based on Hindu or Muslim rites, were not recognized by the colonial state until the 1940s. From the perspective of the planters, a large proportion of women fell in the latter category, which thus exonerated them from their obligations and responsibilities. Many women therefore shouldered familial duties and expenses. Contemporary sociological research gives us some insight as to why there has been a history of gender inequalities in the workplace. The argument is that women in the workplace generally hit the "glass ceiling", an invisible barrier that keeps them from rising to their maximum potential. Additionally, because women's earnings have often been seen by employers as supplemental to the family income, they have been paid lower wages.[20] These attitudes were certainly expressed during the indentured period.

Gender Relations and Social Violence

East Indian emigrants brought with them a concept of gender relations totally different from those of other ethnic groups in the Caribbean. Among the emigrants themselves, there were different expectations of gender relations or gender unions, and this was further complicated by the categories of women (discussed below) who came to the colonies. As so often occurs in traditional society, nineteenth-century Hindu men, when faced with an unfaithful wife or one suspected of marital offences, were likely to treat the situation with violence, often leading to death. If an East Indian wife was raped, she stood a good chance of expulsion from her husband's home. Once married, they were expected to regard, rhapsodize and treat their husbands in accord with the orthodox Hindu tenets. Women were expected to be faithful to their husbands at all times. Adulterous behaviour was often punished with spousal abuse, communities applauding husbands for carrying out such thrashings. In certain parts of India, honour killings were considered justifiable, and husbands generally received sympathy, making it difficult to muster evidence against the murderer.

Reports under the slave period indicated that although the plantation hierarchy tried to suppress some of these deviant cultural practices, some did exist amongst both African and European ethnic groups long before East Indians entered the Caribbean. In the post-emancipation period, the planters strictly opposed these cultural practices in an attempt to forestall social apathies on the plantations. They were bent on recruiting "docile coolies", including women of good moral standing. Such expectations were generally unfulfilled because colonial emigration agents admitted that the scramble for women undoubtedly led recruiters to persons who were not desirable emigrants.[21] Thus, women from various backgrounds entered the Caribbean.

East Indian women recruited for the Caribbean colonies were from three main categories:

1. Single women, although some single women were engaged in relationships while in the depot, on the ship or on the plantation. They comprised the largest proportion of women emigrants.
2. Married women with or without families. Some married women brought their young daughters with them and, according to emigration agents, "it is well known that daughters are regarded by the average Indian family as a doubtful blessing owing to the expenses that have to be incurred in finding husbands for them, and the novel prospect of having their girls sought after by eligible young men in the colonies might be an inducement to them to emigrate".[22]
3. Widows, destitute women abandoning their families and prostitutes drawn from the sprawling metropolises of Calcutta and Madras. The McNeil–Lal report stated that the great majority of women who migrated to the colonies were not, contrary to common opinion, "shamelessly immoral".[23]

This diversity and shortage of women as well as European-dominated work routines and power structures did not allow East Indian homeland cultural values either to materialize or to meliorate in the Caribbean. New and modified forms of gender relationships emerged and evolved. There was a shift in the roles of East Indian women on the plantations from mainly providing family and communal support to satisfying male desires and sexuality. This was partly due to their scarcity, which caused conflicts and the reinforcement of East Indian patriarchal behaviour in the Caribbean. As East Indian men competed for the few East Indian women, the result was violence. From 1859 to 1863, East Indian husbands or reputed husbands murdered sixteen and eleven East Indian women in British Guiana and

Trinidad respectively.²⁴ Mohapatra's calculations from various annual immigration reports of Trinidad and British Guiana suggested that between 1872 and 1879, of 102 total murders, seventy-six were women, of which thirty-nine were wives. Again, between 1898 and 1913, of 102 total murders, thirty-nine were women and eighteen were wives. In British Guiana, between 1885 and 1900, of 103 murders, seventy-eight were women and fifty-eight were wives.²⁵ Wife murders were observed in East Indian communities throughout the Caribbean. Evidence to this effect was often disclosed by various Christian religious denominations in the colonies.

7. A young East Indian female performer. Courtesy of Skeldon Estate, Guyana.

Colonial officials offered two different sets of explanations for the high number of wife murders in the colonies: first, the shortage of women on the plantations and, second, the cultural characteristics of East Indian emigrants. These views were essential in determining how East Indian women were to be treated in the Caribbean. The imperial and colonial governments always believed an increase of East Indian women would reduce anxiety and lead to more stable relationships in East Indian quarters. But, as we have seen, this prospect posed a few challenges, since most "desirable" East Indian women were reluctant to travel long distances, the more vulnerable, low-caste women were the usual recruits.

By contrast, the culturalist view claims that the high rate of wife murder in the colonies was related to the socioeconomic status of the women recruited and the East Indian male view of them rather than to the scarcity of women per se. Much has been ascribed to the concept that East Indian patriarchal norms in the colonies were challenged as women became more conscious about certain avenues of freedom and expression. The planters and missionaries, in particular, embraced the theory that the wife-murder phenomenon in the colonies was a direct social practice transferred from India. They reckoned that East Indian men were predisposed to such acts to resolve social problems, and they were stoically indifferent about the consequences, both for the victims as well as for themselves. Colonial officials claimed that a common remark of an East Indian man when asked in a court of law why he had killed his wife was that he killed no one else's wife but his own.[26]

Two points of contention, however, make the culturist theory myopic and biased. On the one hand, if they were more inclined to resolve social problems with violence, then why were more men not murdered? One must emphasize that it is much easier for a man to kill a woman than another man. On the other hand, the culturalist theory does not adequately explain why the murder rate was so much higher in the Caribbean than in the home environment in India. The number of wife murders between 1866 and 1870 in Madras, Bengal and North Western Provinces, of a population of 25,105,020, 42,865,569 and 26,985,590, were 154, 339 and 148 respectively.[27] Murder rates were much lower in India than in the Caribbean. The hopelessness and the lack of family stability led to promiscuous and irresponsible behaviour,

8. A party for East Indian female pensioners or weeders. Courtesy of Skeldon Estate, Guyana.

but reasons for the high rates of violence among East Indians in the colonies cannot be limited to the shortage of women and the culturalist theory.

The authoritarian structure of the plantation must be taken into consideration to explain the social ills emanating from indentured East Indian Caribbean communities. This system stifled values and culture because its purpose was to extract as much labour as possible from indentured workers, regardless of their social needs and adjustments. In any system where there is a lack of resources to support the emotionally disturbed and depressed, certain values will generally give way to unsettling habits and low standards of morality. Certainly, some aspects of East Indian culture demonstrated this trend. Traditional survival customs became diluted as plantation life became increasingly repressive. For example, the *Panchayat* system (the council of five influential men), which was responsible for solving disputes in India, broke down in the Caribbean under enormous pressure from the plantation system and under a potpourri of new internal problems among indentured servants. Small quarrels subsequently developed into serious crimes. The frustrations and feelings of powerlessness of men, and to some extent women, found outlets in abuse within families and in the larger community.

To understand why such social maladies existed, we have to turn to a few contemporary sociological explanations. Sociologist Walter Reckless developed the control theory to explain the prevention of crime. The theory posits that there are two control systems: inner and outer. The inner control system is regulated by internal moral principles such as conscience and religion, which work to prevent acts of deviance because of the fear of punishment and disappointment imposed on families, friends and the communities. The outer control system is generally one's commitment and engagement to his or her society. So if an individual has weak ties with society – imposed or self-inflicted – there is a possibility for the breakdown of societal norms.[28] The planters certainly cared little for the family life of indentured servants. The rationale they gave to explain East Indian social problems was similar to what modern-day sociologists call techniques of neutralization in delinquency.²⁹ These entail denial of responsibility, denial of injury, denial of victim, condemnation and appeal to higher authorities.³⁰

The explicit manifestations of sexual exploitation or "sexploitation"³¹ of East Indian women were not confined to East Indian men. White colonial men found the bodies of brown East Indian women highly desirable, and these feelings were expressed in the workplace, mainly in the sugar-cane fields where women were more vulnerable. Such modes of conduct were an extension of what had happened under slavery. African-American feminist bell hooks believes that exploitation of colonized women was a practice that was "both right and rite of the white male dominating group" on the plantations.³² White male overseers were seldom married and depended on East Indian women to satisfy their wants, desires and excesses. Few women were able to resist sexual advances from white overseers and myriad circumstances existed where overseers singled out Hindu women for an Arabian night's entertainment in the Caribbean. Leslie Phillips, an overseer at *Plantation Cornelia Ida* in British Guiana, provides one chilling example of an oppressive relationship between white colonial men and East Indian women. In some of his memories of sugar plantation life, which he titled *Single Men in Barracks,* he writes:

> This involved Rajama, a comely but slightly promiscuous young Madrasi whose husband was complacent and indolent. The latter found more gratification in rum-drinking than in any other pleasure, and by mutual consent each permitted the other unquestioned choice of leisure activities. Their ideas of entertainment differed: she being interested in the body and he in the spirit, so to speak. Thus it was that Rajama spent one Saturday night in my quarters, and daylight taking us unawares, we decided to let the next nightfall cover her journey home.
>
> About two o'clock on Sunday afternoon my house-boy brought the ominous news that Rajama's husband had arrived and wished to speak to her. To permit this would have placed me in open jeopardy, so I sought means to distract him. Learning of my predicament, Brown, a fellow Overseer, offered to get the man completely drunk if I would supply the liquor. I sent my boy with a chit to Fung-a-Fat's Rum Shop, and he quickly returned with a large bottle of rum which Brown invited the man to share in his room.³³

Jamaican social historian Verene Shepherd found evidence that East Indian women were sexually exploited even before they entered the Caribbean colonies. She reiterated that they, like African women before them, were sexually abused on the sea voyage to the Caribbean. These acts were interconnected with "racist and sexist traditions" imposed on the Caribbean judicial system. Shepherd concluded that "elite men who dominated the legal system were affected by the prevailing stereotypes and characterization of non-European women as people of loose character and questionable morals".[34]

How did the indentured community deal with such exploitation? For the most part, indentured East Indian communities sought various means to resolve the social ills associated with the sexual disparity in the population. One East Indian woman generally shared several East Indian men in exchange for extra rations and protection, while some men cohabited with other men. The plantation provided fertile grounds for exploitation, with planters providing few opportunities for a stable family life. Its very political and social structure denigrated and ridiculed East Indians, pushing them into powerless positions. East Indian women, however, were still subjected to further gender oppression. For example, some East Indian parents sold their daughters to wealthy East Indian men old enough to be their fathers in order to collect bride price.[35] One father sold his three daughters at a lucrative price and returned to India with more than £1,000 and a fair amount of jewellery.[36]

Another interesting point should be discussed in this section since it is characteristic of the overall attitude of East Indian men under indentured servitude. Despite the shortage of East Indian women, sexual unions or relationships between East Indian men and African women were rare. After the first two decades of the indenture system, the Protector of Immigrants to Trinidad was able to quantify that there was not a single instance of an indentured immigrant who cohabited with an African. It is interesting to note that by the last decades of the indenture system such attitudes changed only marginally. For example, in Suriname between 1892 and 1917, there were on average about two interracial marriages a year, mostly between Africans and East Indians. The record shows that no interracial marriage occurred between East Indians and Javanese.[37] This was not surprising because East Indians were socialized along the values of caste endogamy.

Therefore, East Indian men were inclined to have sexual relationships with women from other ethnic backgrounds, but were reluctant to take them as wives. They feared caste and social exclusion from fellow indentured servants if they intermarried with women from other ethnic groups. Whatever might have been the real cause for the lack of interracial unions between Africans and East Indians, the offspring of these multi-racial unions were viewed with contempt and even with a sense of utter shame, particularly in the East Indian communities. For example, a child from an African/East Indian union is still called a *doogla* (hybrid) in the British Caribbean and is considered to be an outcast in mainstream Caribbean East Indian communities.[38] The following folk song among early indentured servants testifies to this reprehension:

> As the hot spices mixed into the dal
> So mixed the makrat and the coolie girl
> And produce the mongrel children.[39]

East Indian Women and the Third Space

One of the most interesting analytical themes of Indo-Caribbean women history was whether their experience under the indenture system emancipated them or created a new form of dependence. Rhoda Reddock argues it was a sign of independence and autonomy that a majority of single women chose to emigrate.[40] She reiterates that the intentions of indentured East Indian women were to serve out their contracts, to improve their social and economic position and to remain in the host society. Reddock, however, confirms that they were repressed or "denied freedom" during indenture through the stranglehold of the planters, the East Indian patriarchal system, the colonial authority and various religious organizations. Ravindra Jain challenges these formulations, and states that Reddock's "ideas about caste status and social origins of immigrant women are confused and contradictory".[41]

Peiter Emmer proposes more convincingly that most East Indian women emigrated willingly, and the indenture system gave women the choice between field work and staying home ("housewifization", a term used by Reddock). He also posits that female East Indian indentured servants in Suriname used the contract system more than men "to increase their social status and to emancipate themselves from an illiberal, inhibiting and very hierarchical social system in India".⁴² Brian Moore claims that indentured East Indian women in British Guiana controlled their social and sexual lives, and "it was not uncommon either for a woman to leave a man with whom she was living for another, then for a third, and perhaps for a fourth and sometimes return to one of those whom she had previously deserted".⁴³ There is no denying that they moved from one male partner to another, but one has to take into consideration the circumstances that caused them to exhibit this behaviour in the first place and whether this behaviour constituted freedom and independence.

While these opposite views offer some insights into the position of indentured East Indian women and certainly has contributed to reducing the paucity of East Indian historiography in the Caribbean, they, at the same time, valorize the dominant Western discourse. Colonial discourse has construed history and human relationships in the pedagogy of binary opposites: West and East; good and evil; black and white; margin and centre; uncivilized and civilized; unequal and equal; bound and free. Very rarely have the concepts of colonial discourse taken into consideration that the position of the subaltern class can be articulated or determined between extremes, and that subaltern groups can produce their own accounts of their history, or that their history can be perceived through a middle ground – or the Third Space. Much of the same misreading has been applied to the position of indentured East Indian women in the Caribbean. Indeed, while some of these women benefited from the indenture system and others were castigated by it, some existed between these extremes. In reconstructing their position under indenture, one has to be careful not to invite or justify the extension of colonial discourse. As Raymond Williams and Edward Said point out, we "need to unlearn the inherent dominative modes" when examining the past.⁴⁴ In the absence of any theoretical strategy about how East Indian women fared under the indenture system, the historical analysis has usually been given from the perspective of the planters' class. The struggles – and even the achievements – of East Indian women were defined by the dominant class. Writing on the position of East Indian women in Suriname, Emmer states that while African women maintained their West African values, rights to posses land, divorce and independence "all this was alien to Indian society".⁴⁵ Reddock offers somewhat similar conclusions when she asserts that "wage differentials in most instances served the traditional purpose of making Indian women dependent on men in spite of the fact that they were full time workers".⁴⁶ These analyses have not provided us with an adequate explanation about how East Indian women used their terrain to articulate their positions, bound or free, under the indenture system. We have seen a body of primary-level analysis, but the secondary level, that is, when efforts are made to reconstitute a subaltern group on a theoretical basis, how they saved and restored their sense of survival and their community against pressures from an authoritarian colonial system, is yet to be embraced.

Writing on the history of women in colonial India, Gayatri Spivak shows that the position of East Indian women was subjected to double oppression or double colonization, caught between the domination of East Indian patriarchy and European masculine-imperialist ideology. Ironically, their position in East Indian society was further complicated by the fact that European masculinism was more powerful than East Indian patriarchy.⁴⁷ The British regarded some East Indian customs, especially *sati*, with contempt, born out of ignorance and fear. It was believed that white men were saving brown women from brown men and from brute practices of *sati*, although some Christian churches in Europe were still burning women suspected of witchcraft activities in the late eighteenth century.⁴⁸ The British saw most East Indian men as innocuous, while the women were considered both sexually predatory and submissive. Much of the same attitude was ascribed to East Indian indentured servants in the Caribbean. But, there were differences.

In India, the British used the rigid caste structure to justify control and colonization. They embraced the notion that there was a spiritual link between Brahman Hinduism and Europeans. This very link allowed them to have control over different tribal groups and communities in India, essentially holding millions of East Indians in fixed and marginal positions. As long as the East Indian patriarchy did not interfere with the British colonial project in India, it was allowed to perpetuate and manifest itself in East Indian society. These power structures defined the way women saw themselves. While some of this was transferred to the Caribbean, the function of caste as a matter of control played a secondary role (see chapter 3) to class and colour. By colonial customs and laws, any person with light skin or of European descent, regardless of economic standing or intellectual ability, enjoyed a status that was superior to that of anyone with black or brown skin. These views denigrated anyone whose class and colour was non-European or anyone whose status was associated with menial labour. East Indians entered the Caribbean with these characteristics. Being brown-skinned and working as indentured servants, they were automatically relegated to the lowest stratum of Caribbean society. But it was within this Third Space between European imperialist patriarchy at the top and East Indian patriarchy at the bottom that the position of indentured East Indian women can best be articulated. The Third Space was a place of agency and intervention, and where cultural meaning was located as well as constructed. It was also a place where East Indian indentured women created a sense of identity. Interestingly, it did not create anything new or anything original; rather, it was a space where culture – especially suppressed cultural characteristics – was expressed. According to post-colonial theorist Homi Bhabha, the Third Space

> may open the way to conceptualizing an international culture, based not on the exoticism of multiculturalism or the diversity of cultures, but on the inscription and articulation of culture hybridity. To that end we should remember that it is the 'inter' – cutting edge of translation and negotiation, the in-between space – that carries the burden of the meaning of culture. It makes it possible to begin envisaging national, anti-nationalistic histories of the 'people'. And by exploring this Third Space, we may elude the politics of polarity and emerge as the others of ourselves.[49]

Central to the interpretation of resistance and accommodation of indentured East Indian women was the concept of hybridity, which in this context means syncretism and duplication. In terms of resistance and accommodation, hybridity generally divides power and creates a space of ambivalence in which there is no actual control of power. Hybridity shifts and displaces power, and in the process nothing is repressed but merely repeated; "the presence of power is revealed as something other than what its rules of recognition assert".⁵⁰ Nowhere are hybridity and resistance of East Indian women more visible than in the practice of *Matikor* – an all-female celebration of female sexuality on the Friday night of a Hindu wedding. This cultural practice was transferred from India to the Caribbean. According to one account, it was believed that *Matikor* was started by East Indian eunuchs, called *hijras*. Since eunuchs were not brought to the Caribbean, the tradition was taken over by young indentured brides. Not only were they the carriers and preservers of *Matikor*, but they also used this celebration to deal plantation domination. Rosanne Kanhai writes:

> *Matikor* provided a rare opportunity for plantation and post-plantation women to claim a space of celebration and articulation. Adorning themselves with their best clothing, face decoration and jewelry . . . women could give themselves the beauty and dignity denied to them in the rigors of daily life. They shared gossip and jokes, sang traditional songs and performed dances that were celebratory and sexually suggestive. *Matikor* was a place of healing where women could act out their resistance against the degradation and depersonalization imposed upon them by the ruling class.⁵¹

The reader should know that at *Matikor*, East Indian women engaged in, among other things, provocative dancing, especially the circular movement of the waist ("wine") or pelvic gyrations. To an outsider, these acts might appear innocuous, but for these women they are the impetus for social intercourse which exemplifies individuality and control. These acts are intended to inform the would-be bride (particularly if she is a virgin) as to what lies ahead and to reverse the role of patriarchy. The *Matikor* ceremony is a ritual place for East Indian women to express themselves. This place where they were dominant was private and unrecorded.

During *Matikor* celebrations, East Indian women created complex palimpsests of hybridization or duality (female/male sexuality) that indicated they were never suppressed and silenced by patriarchy in absolute terms. Instead, *Matikor* demonstrated that they developed new anti-monolithic models of cultural exchange and growth. Hybridization created new modes of differentiation and new sites of power for resistance, and "turns the discursive conditions of dominance into grounds of intervention".⁵² In the ritual, provocative circular movement of the waist reveals and mimics, to some degree, what some East Indian women experience in a patriarchal setting (bedroom). Their actions signify that they have become "mimic women", essentially renouncing imposed male dominant traits in acting like their oppressor. As Jenny Sharpe points out, to resemble is to threaten the base of power and discrimination, and the mimic individuals are contradictory figures who simultaneously reinforce as well as disturb colonial authority.[53] The effectiveness of this strategy is that the oppressor becomes displaced as he sees himself in the other, the oppressed. This process disrupts normalized knowledge and disciplinary power because it confuses the oppressor and generates ambivalence. Consequently, authoritative power is thwarted. The duplicity of mimicry produces an effective representation of resistance. By being like the oppressor (European patriarchy or East Indian patriarchy) through *Matikor*, East Indian women displaced power. The celebration of the ritual also created ambivalence and contradictory modes of representation, particularly among East Indian men, mainly because it was not fixed and pre-known. Domination and power need a fixed target in order to have control. *Matikor* celebrations produced a sense of comfort, acknowledgement and pleasure. In this context, substitution reduced fear of loss and feelings of inferiority, built confidence and generated a sense of control.

Conclusion

Previous studies rightly stressed that indentured servitude was a modified form of slavery, it implied victimization. Indentured servants were ridiculed and maltreated in the depot, on the voyage and on the sugar plantations. This was not surprising because the very society that had abolished slavery also governed indentured servitude. Fashioned in a belief system that for more than three centuries saw nothing wrong with slavery, it was easy to conclude that this society found nothing unjust in bonded labour. East Indian indentured servants seemed to possess all the requisite characteristics of former slaves. Not only were they supposedly docile and desultory, but more importantly, they were dark-skinned and therefore fitted the vital criterion upon which exploitation was rationalized – inferior and suited for tropical labour.[1] To select otherwise would have created political and social disorder, because the colonial economy depended on forced and controlled labour.

Indentured servitude was oppressive, and the individuals who directed and safeguarded the system were interested only in changing the form of forced labour, not its substance. Magistrate Des Voeux of British Guiana, in a letter to Sir Clinton Murdoch, chairman of the British and Emigration Commissioners, declared that the magistrates, emigration agents and even the governors were receptive and subservient to the views of planters and indifferent to the plight of indentured servants. He stated further that there was "a cruel neglect of duty" and "perversion of justice" in the colonies.² Surely, indentured servants were poorly treated in their homeland, but they traded their liberty but did not gain freedom, since many did know and experience freedom. Indentured servants wanted protection and, most of all, to be beneficiaries of indentured servitude, not victims.

The colonial government encouraged emigration and the establishment of settled East Indian communities, but hardly provided a positive environment for the development of a settled domestic life. This neglect caused desertion and high mortality rates. The colonial government restored population levels through further recruitment of East Indians. Additionally, alcoholism, sexual violence, wife chopping, murder and suicides were widespread on plantation estates worked by East Indians, more so than among other ethnic groups in the Caribbean. Victorian officials and missionaries were convinced that something was peculiarly awkward with them, especially East Indian men. They opined that they had a proclivity for solving social problems with violence. Hardly ever did the plantation management take into consideration that the indentured servants were coming to grips with the capitalist norms of time and labour discipline imposed on them. Some found plantation work unbearable and even more were deeply disturbed by the restrictions placed on their cultural and physical mobility. Indentured servants were not allowed to leave the plantation without a pass, and even the time-expired indentured servants had to produce evidence of being discharged from contractual agreements. They did not have the right to demand higher wages or refuse work allocated to them. Estate managers were often described as individuals who had no feelings.

The endurance and the adaptive capacity of these indentured Indians – amid one of the most severe labour regimens conceivable – must be measured alongside their sufferings. Walter Rodney showed how Europe underdeveloped Africa,³ while Eric Williams demonstrated how slavery contributed to the development of the capitalist economy.⁴ Likewise, we have already noted how indentured service led to some extent to the underdevelopment of its servants. We can equally surmise that they contributed to the world economy and to the success of capitalism. Indentured servitude made up for the deficiencies of the capitalist economy, especially when Caribbean sugar was faced with stiff competition from European beet sugar, especially after the demise of slavery. Thus, the history of specific Caribbean countries, Guyana and Trinidad for example, cannot be written without understanding of the contributions of East Indians.

In the late nineteenth century, James Stark wrote that since the arrival of East Indians in Trinidad "commerce has taken wonderful strides, the export of sugar has increased five fold and that of cacao three fold".[5] Rodway showed that this achievement was possible because of the supply of East Indian indentured servants.[6] As a result, British West Indian exports rose by 21.1 per cent in 1895, much greater than in 1828. In 1828, 193,069 tons of sugar were produced, compared to 235,292 in 1895. The increase in sugar production was particularly noticeable in British Guiana and Trinidad where a larger number of East Indian indentured emigrants worked. Grenada, St Vincent, St Kitts and Jamaica, places that all received comparatively fewer indentured servants, experienced a decline in sugar exports.[7] These statistics suggest that the large influx of East Indian indentured servants in British Guiana and Trinidad were directly related to the increase of sugar exports and the maintenance of the sugar industry, while in smaller islands the reverse was evident.

Similar developments were also noticed in the rice industry. Although Africans introduced rice cultivation in the Caribbean, it was East Indians who developed this industry, essentially wet rice cultivation, a tradition they brought from India. Moreover, rice cultivation enabled many East Indians to survive a low-wage regime and raise a substantial part of their own food supply.[8] Equally important was that rice cultivation provided an economic base for East Indians, and profits from it were much greater than from the cultivation of ground crops. By World War I, British Guiana had begun to export rice.[9] Stembridge reminds us that "as a rice grower, the coolie has achieved results which constitute a romance of tropical life. At one time British Guiana imported all her rice. That importation has almost ceased, and in its place, there has developed an export which in eight years increases in value from £60 to £60,000."[10] Small wonder then that Caribbean novelist George Lamming says that East Indians' industrious hands continue to feed the Caribbean.[11]

But what about the indentured servants? Did they benefit from this system? As noted, defects and deficiencies in the system were multiple, but alongside this, there were comparative material improvements. A majority of East Indian indentured servants were better off in the Caribbean than in India considering that, over time, many became proprietors of small plots of land. Land ownership provided the base for economic and social mobility. Moreover, some East Indians who stayed in the Caribbean accumulated substantial savings, though many went back empty-handed. One feature of East Indian custom that has been consistently overlooked was their material inconspicuousness. All East Indians looked equal in economic standing because they were meticulous about not exposing their wealth, a habit common in rural villages in India. They believe that exposure of wealth invites *dacoits* (or robbers) and, more importantly, requests from poor relatives and friends for money.[12] This practice was more noticeable during the period of indentureship rather than in contemporary society. Thus, the following statistics on savings and remittances East Indians took back to India do not tell the whole story of their financial achievements in the Caribbean. After indenture, wealth was very noticeable among East Indians, especially among the rural rice planting elite and business retailers.

By 1911–1912, there were 8,214 East Indian depositors at the Government Savings Bank in British Guiana with savings totalling £123,051. In Trinidad, for the same period, the savings of East Indians totalled £81,403. From 1890 to 1912, this group in British Guiana and Trinidad remitted £52,975 and £65,187 to India, respectively.[13] One must bear in mind that the average weekly wage of indentured servants at this time was less than £1. Although interesting, the statistics on savings are not accurate for two main reasons. First, East Indians were suspicious about banks and preferred to have someone else to keep their money or to store it in bed mattresses, hollow trees or holes in the ground.[14] Some older generation East Indians still practise this habit in the Caribbean and will withdraw their money from the bank just to make sure that it is there. In his novel *Corentyne Thunder*, Edgar Mittelholzer writes about Ramgolall, the cow minder, who preferred to save his money and go sick instead of paying for medical attention.[15] Some East Indians are still thrifty in the Caribbean, but more for family values than anything else. East Indians will make sacrifices – eat less, spend less and save more – in order to secure a better future for their children. Second, they still prefer to invest their money in jewellery rather than in the bank. This behaviour was brought over from India where the practice still goes on, especially among low-caste East Indians. Ironically, the habit of investing in gold has enabled them to survive unstable Caribbean economies, as in Guyana during the period of cooperative socialism.

Similar achievements were noticed in land ownership. During 1910–1911, for example, 290 East Indians in British Guiana received transports or titles for property at a value of $71,578.[16] Around the same period in Suriname, over 200,000 acres of land went to indentured servants, either free, leased or purchased. The practice of conceding parcels of land to indentured servants was advantageous to the colonial government because it saved repatriation and replacement costs. But this policy was also realized at the expense of Africans.

Land ownership and inherent parsimony set the foundation from which many East Indian communities were moulded. As their material standing improved, some moved off the plantations and accepted occupations elsewhere, as in the civil service. Others grabbed the opportunity to buy farmlands and pursue agricultural activities alongside government-owned industries. Thus, a generation of East Indians grew up, some in relative prosperity, others using educational opportunities to improve themselves further. Soon after indenture emancipation (1920), they began to accept the Caribbean as their home. The following folk songs in Suriname underlined East Indian appreciation of the Caribbean:

> The city of Hansu (village outside Paramaribo) is a flourishing one, my brother;
> (And) the habitation there is unending.
> In Paramaribo, across (the river from the) city, my brother,
> Now, there is established a market-place (full) of love.
> O, an estate like Maryamburg (I) have not seen (elsewhere),
> (Where I have a) shop in front of the office.
> have not seen cows (so good elsewhere) as in Hansu
> Where (there is an) open right to pasturage.

And, East Indians discouraged fellow East Indians from leaving the Caribbean:

> Young man, do not go abroad.
> I and you will be able to manage (together) right here;
> Young man . . .
> Yours and my love is waxing strong; I shall die crying and crying.
> The water of the foreign lands is infectious; one dies immediately upon drinking it.
> The women of the foreign lands are bad; they glance and put magic on you.
> Young man, do not go abroad.[17]

Some studies have argued that the achievements made during indenture were exaggerated.[18] They claim that the system caused more harm than good and refer to particulars already mentioned. But let us examine the indenture system in retrospect.

Certainly, the kidnapping, luring, duping and so on, in order to convert East Indians to indenture service are well known; that is now well-established. But there were those who came voluntarily and worked the plantations and even re-indentured themselves for a second, and even third, time. This trend was partly influenced by return emigrants.

Indentured servitude gave poor East Indians an opportunity to improve their lot through migration. They have always migrated; many still do, in and around India, especially seeking work. The migration to overseas destinations like the Caribbean was markedly different, however. Work codes, standards and expectations were more or less the same in and around India, particularly with regard to the caste system, which arguably crippled any opportunity for personal economic and social advancement. The Caribbean plantation system, including its authoritative and repressive characteristics, was different in that it did not allow occupational roles to revolve around caste doctrines. Even land purchase shows that there was no significant difference between the high and low castes. Among the Caribbean East Indian population, caste was not an important determinant for land acquisition.[19] This is one of the reasons why East Indians were able to achieve a measure of success in the Caribbean.

Of paramount importance was that every indentured servant entered the Caribbean on an equal footing regardless of religion, caste or gender, a phenomenon most indentured servants never had experienced before. While equality was thwarted on the plantations, because of the nature of the plantation system and the determination of Brahmans to reassert their superiority, a number of low-caste East Indians were able to improve their lives through indentured service. Their development and progress are not hard to pinpoint. In India, many were little different from slaves to their landlords for life. Many also could not feed themselves because of hardships and famine. The planters did not provide adequate rations for their indentured servants, but starvation and famine, at least to the same degree as in India, was unknown in the Caribbean. Equally important was that the position of indentured servants was not fixed, especially time-expired indentured servants and, after their emancipation in 1920, they had, at least in theory, access to the same opportunities as other ethnic groups in the Caribbean. Furthermore, the steady influx of indentured servants is evidence that there might have been something good with the system.

Although research in the Caribbean has recently begun to retrieve voices from indentured servants to determine what actually transpired during this period, a folk song from an indentured servant from Fiji provides an impression that there were some positive aspects:

> Born in India, we are prepared to go to Fiji
> Or, if you please, to Natal to dig the mines
> We are prepared to suffer there,
> But Brothers! Don't make us labourers here [India].[20]

This folk song may not be representative of the attitudes of all indentured servants, but it demonstrates that the experience was not uniformly good or bad for everyone. Despite how hard the system might have been, indentured servants were guaranteed employment and fringe benefits such as rations and medical care, incentives many had never experienced before.

But how were some indentured servants able to achieve a measure of success against a system repeatedly labelled as monstrous, and one that had failed to protect them from the worst forms of abuse? A number of studies have shown that East Indian resistance was based on "cultural resilience and adaptation".[21] Strategies of resistance were perpetrated through traditional culture and the psychological expectation of returning home. Indentured service was seen as temporary, not perpetual, and the day of freedom was foreseeable. Other methods of resistance were actuated through strikes, riots, foot dragging, feigned sickness and so on. While these strategies challenged the indenture system, they were met equally with bullying and cunning acts from the planter class. Consequently, it appeared that indentured servants were pushed into passive and submissive roles. Behind every physical act of resistance, rebellion or revolt, a hidden plan lies waiting. It is this enclosed network (hidden transcript) that we must penetrate in order to understand how the subordinate class generally resisted the vicissitudes of domination and thus coping with and cultivating their lives.

In examining indentured servants' hidden transcripts we can see how they perceived the hidden transcript of the dominant class, and how they used this knowledge to deal with everyday forms of oppression. This technique was instrumental in providing the tools for indentured servants to improve their lives. In symbolically resisting the political and social ideology of the dominant class, they gained a sense of agency to indentured servants. Their compliance was employed so skilfully that it projected a false sense of conformity and acceptance of domination and suppression, when in reality it was a secure strategy of resistance. The strategy was effective for two reasons: because it never appeared to overthrow or threaten the indenture system and because it required little coordination or planning. It is for this reason that the plantation system perceived the indentured servants as docile, lacking any effective leadership. Misunderstood by the dominant class, indentured servants were not interested in changing the power relations – recognizing that this was unlikely – but in using the system to their advantage to enhance and make their life better. One important aspect of symbolic resistance is that the subordinate may "play fool to know wise", because it agrees with the expectations of the dominant class. For domination to be effective, or for it to be known, much depends on the habits of deference and subservience from the subordinate class. As discussed earlier in chapter 2, the high-caste East Indian relies on the conformity of the untouchables and other low castes for the practice of purity to be exercised. Likewise, the untouchable has to be able to read the mood of the high caste and be prepared to adapt to that mood. Over time, the oppressed worked out ways to deal with the oppressor and yet be something else. Indentured servants played this role of resistance and survival through humour, rumour, folk songs and storytelling. These strategies strengthened group cohesion and group solidarity. They were the main arsenal indentured servants used to cope with domination, to alter the impact of the dominant class. They were the conduit through which indentured servants released suppressed feelings, diverted their sufferings and accommodated themselves without renouncing who they were.

The capacity of indentured servants to retain certain homeland cultural features in the face of a hostile plantation environment was remarkable. Hinduism and Islam helped East Indians withstand hard times and guide their daily actions. These two religions provided the indentured servant with inspiration, reassurance and psychological protection in times of doubt and tribulation. Yet their willingness to dispense with other cultural elements cannot be overlooked. The attenuation of the caste system, whether as a result of plantation pressure or the initiative of indentured servants themselves, was one of the main reasons East Indians in the Caribbean were able to achieve a level of social and economic advancement. Even though the caste system in India reportedly has been going through significant changes as a result of industrialization and urbanization, one doubts whether some descendants of indentured servants would have been in a better position in India than in the Caribbean.

It would be interesting to examine repatriated East Indians against those who stayed in the Caribbean. One observer writes that through religion the Brahmans have a hold over the East Indian population in India: "the caste system . . . has kept the people from advancing and has checked the march of civilization".[22] Although they reasserted their religious monopoly over East Indian communities, the Brahmans' importance with regard to purity and the hierarchy of social and economic interdependence was not as pronounced in the Caribbean as in India. Through the process of cultural change and continuity, the status of low-caste indentured servants improved markedly, from the periphery to the centre. For centuries, low-caste East Indians were relegated to the bottom of the social, economic and political sphere of society in India, with no opportunity to escape this bondage. No one denies the persistent poverty among a large number of Caribbean East Indians and the prejudice against them, particularly from the East Indian communities themselves. But no one can deny either the personal advancement of low-caste East Indians. All ranks were able to occupy important positions in the Caribbean beyond the sugar plantations, ranging from cattle owners to clerks, mechanics, shop-keepers, lawyers, doctors, leaders and priests. This was possible particularly because they were freed from the bonds of East Indian society, as expressed by the following remark:

> His social education becomes meaningless to him in new surroundings. He sees the principles which that education inculcates in him daily set at nought by the rest of the population. His confidence in those restrictions and rules which form so much of the Hindu social life is rudely shaken.[23]

Indentured East Indian women also benefited from having personal restrictions limited. Particularly, indentured service created for women a social horizon in which to develop new roles, and they functioned differently beyond their immediate surroundings. They moved beyond the household and made meaningful contact with wider society. They earned wages and had control over their individual lives. Shortages in the Caribbean allowed women a degree of bargaining power and thus further freedom. Yet many indentured women were subdued and suppressed into submissive non-asserting personal roles. They were unable to throw off entirely the shackles of East Indian patriarchy and European masculine ideology. Consequently, they suffered the dual burden of plantation life and were often blamed for the social ills associated with indentured service. They were forced to use alternative strategies to improve their lives. One significant strategy was to exploit the space between East Indian patriarchy and European masculine ideology. Strategies of hybridity and mimicry allowed indentured women to substitute fears and feelings of inferiority for confidence and self-determination.

Indentured servitude was abolished in 1920. Even at the end of the nineteenth century, however, there is evidence that official attitudes were beginning to acknowledge the inherent inhumanity and indefensibility of the system. But, by then, there was already a noticeable shift in the servants' perspective away from the confines of the plantation system to an environment where they could realize personal achievements. For instance, Surgeon-Major Comins of the Indian Immigration Service at Calcutta visited the Caribbean in the 1890s in response to the planters' agitation and to report on the status of the working and living conditions of indentured servants. In his report, he recorded the following poem from British Guiana, which highlighted some positive aspects of the indenture system:

> Oh cooly girl with eyes of wonder!
> With thoughtful brow and lips compressed!
> I know not where your thoughts do wander;
> I know not where your heart doth rest.
>
> Is it far away by rolling Indus?
> Or down by Ganges' sacred wave?
> Or where the lonesome Indian Ocean
> The shores of Malabar doth lave?
>
> Ah no! those lands you never saw!
> This western world claimed your birth;
> Your parents thence their life may draw,
> Their thoughts of joy – their themes of mirth.
>
> This land of mud has been your home,
> 'Twas here you drew your natal breath,
> Your home of childhood – doomed to be
> The land shall hold your dust at death.
>
> Then why so foreign? Why so strange
> In looks and manner, style and dress –
> Religion, too, and social way?
> The mystery I cannot guess.
>
> You dwell so very near a church,
> A Christian church, with tolling bell;
> You never enter it, alas!
> For marriage peal or funeral knell.
>
> A cooly temple far away,
> Pagoda-shaped, with colours loud;
> 'Tis there you wend your stately steps,
> Arrayed in winsome gauzy shroud.

Your parents have been thrifty folks,
And now you scorn a life of toil;

No "Creole gang", no whip, no thong,
Thy youthful beauty e'er does spoil.

Thy father is a landlord now
With herds of cattle, flocks of sheep;
A veritable lady thou,
Thy father's flocks and herds doth keep.

This land is yours, go up, possess!
'Tis here for you to cultivate.
Many have come, many have gone;
They all have left it desolate.

The Carib, Negro, Portuguese,
The Chinaman (not he of delf),
They all have tried their hands, and now
They leave it mostly to yourself.

"Out of running" all of them,
Mere loiterers on the world's highway;
They all are "going, going, gone",
The cooly man has come to stay.

The future of this land is yours; . . .[24]

For over eighty years (1838–1920) East Indian indentured servants persistently sought to improve and better their lives on the Caribbean sugar plantations. Despite the despotic and deceptive nature of the system, which followed on the heels of slavery, they were not really its victims but "victors". They had manipulated the system with limited resources to improve their lot. Certainly, no one understates or underestimates the colonial regime's ability to execute and maintain the exploitative nature of the plantation system. Nevertheless, within its ambit of power and control, indentured servants found their niche and methods of resistance, using techniques which, in many respects, were not easily recognizable. Specifically, they resisted domination, reproduced and re-invented their culture, adapted themselves, and turned adverse circumstances to their advantage. This study also bears witness to other works which address the subject of East Indian victimization under the indenture system. It has been argued here that indentured servants used the system of victimization to establish protective barriers against domination and fashioned ways beneficial to them. This historical attitude of resistance and adaptation provided the skills East Indians used to build their post-indenture communities. As under the indenture system, their struggle for survival and identity in a predominantly multiethnic, creolized Caribbean society continues, as Kelvin Singh points out in his study *Race and Class Struggles in a Colonial State: Trinidad 1917–1945*. Resistance, adaptation and accommodation have become institutionalized into the socioeconomic fabric of Caribbean East Indians. And if ever there is a connection between indenture and the contemporary period, it is the East Indian's own internal dynamics of resistance and accommodation.

Appendices

Appendix 1	122
Appendix 2	124
Appendix 3	126
Appendix 4	127
Appendix 5	128
Appendix 6	129
Appendix 7	130
Appendix 8	131
Appendix 9	132
Appendix 10	134
Appendix 11	135

Appendix 1

Emigrants from Calcutta, India, to and from the Colonies

Years	Mauritius migration to	Mauritius migration from	Demerara migration to	Demerara migration from	Trinidad migration to	Trinidad migration from	Jamaica migration to	Jamaica migration from	Grenada migration to	Grenada migration from	St Lucia migration to	St Lucia migration from	St Kitts migration to	St Kitts migration from	Natal migration to	Natal migration from
1842	459															
1843	17,653	642														
1844	7,171	602														
1845	8,542	803	1,359		1,332		1,047									
1846	7,180	1,451	1,416		755		780									
1847	5,813	1,417	1,519		619		540									
1848	5,667	1,698	1,024	2	680											
1849	7,858	3,326														
1850	5,944	2,855														
1851	6,948	2,865	1,927	244	1,094	20										
1852	7,994	2,598	2,351	645	1,729	364										
1852–54	7,994	3,682	2,653	218	1,497	487										
1854–55	10,218	2,202	2,321	245	294											
1855–56	8,590	3,763	949		623	290										
1856–57	3,531	3,198	988		1,561	308			364							
1857–58	11,250	3,532	1,091	565	1,451				382							
1858–59	22,499	5,187	2,462	309	2,173				332							
1859–60	17,606	2,873	4,594	378	1,736	355	703									
1860–61	6,091	1,778	4,288		2,080		1,709				361					
1861–62	6,936	1,421	4,366		2,030	289	2,161		1,122						610	
1862–63	2,284	1,714	2,967	398	1,389											
1863–64	1,822	2,144	2,643		1,433											
1864–65	6,868	2,463	6,139	414	1,450	492										
1865–66	15,117	2,861	2,842	394	1,498				285						481	
1866–67	478	2,047	4,509		2,993		1,705									
1867–68	313	1,797	3,001	397	1,840											
1868–69	1,237	1,446	5,014		1,498	1	1,426									
1869–70	1,499	974	6,685	418	2,993	369	924				75					
1870–71	1,937	1,588	3,199	416	2,087	393	1,382				274					
1871–72	2,990	1,700	2,125	434	1,620	157	1,279	898								
1872–73	5,262	2,068	6,087	846	2,850		1,562	400								
1873–74	5,387	1,522	8,497	473	2,138	376	1,463				110					
1874–75	4,914	1,837	3,943	900	2,540	405	1,258									
1875–76	739	1,782	3,849	443	1,653	2	767	268							6,025	
1876–77	1,027	1,326	3,992	868	1,601	485		247							393	139
1877–78	2,034	1,284	8,288	489	2,151	459	896	307	461						761	5
1878–79	1,220	1,402	6,520	1,599	2,632		165	227							1,734	36
1879–80	539	1,602	4,498	1,118	3,161	473	756	407								
1880–81	235	1,502	4,416	1,566	3,342	446	513	361			29				980	97
1881–82		849	3,168	970	2,591	456		399							1,260	187
1882–83	994	1,206	2,974	978	1,963	456	398	442							878	48
Total	232,802	80,007	126,656	15,727	66,769	7,190	21,434	5,188	3,220		214		361		14,214	517

Sources: Tabulated from various primary and secondary sources. See House of Commons, *Parliamentary Papers* 1910, 1914; House of Commons, *Parliamentary Papers, The General Report of the Colonial Land and Emigration Commissioners* (London: HMSO, 1854–1870); IOR, *India Emigration Proceedings*, 1885; G.W. Roberts and J. Byrne, "Summary Statistics on Indenture and Associated Migration Affecting the West Indies, 1834–1918", *Population Studies* 20 (1966): 125–34; Keith Laurence, *A Question of Labor: Indentured Immigration into Trinidad and British Guiana, 1875–1917* (New York: St Martin's Press, 1994); Walton Look Lai, *Indentured Labor, Caribbean Sugar: Chinese and Indian Migrants to the*

Appendix 1 (continued)

	St Vincent		Nevis		Fiji		Reunion		Cayene		Guadeloupe		Martinque		St Croix		Surinam	
	migration to	migration from	migration to	migration from	migration to	migration from	migration to	migration from	migration to	migration from	migration to	migration from	migration to	migration from	migration to	migration from	migration to	migration from
	316				5,339													
					864													
					291	4												
					1,627													
	233																	
	490						278											
							322											
	349																	
		294																
	332															250		
		32																
															410			
			342						1,427		441		1,350		3,528			
	342										521		1,209					
				40									1,329					
													353					
													2,361				324	
					498								2,166				709	
	213						189						1,685				320	798
		165											1,413				965	
		78											1,002				496	
		71			922		192					46	986	169			45	
	2,275	680	342		1,420		8,115		985	1,427	962	46	13,854	169	312	250	6,792	798

British West Indies, 1838–1917 (Baltimore: Johns Hopkins University Press, 1993); Verene Shepherd, *Transients to Settlers: The Experience of Indians in Jamaica, 1845–1950* (Leeds: Peepal Tree Press, 1994); Steve Vertovec, *Hindu Trinidad: Religion, Ethnicity and Socio-Economic Change* (London: Macmillan, 1992); Rosemarijin Hoefte, *In Place of Slavery: A Social History of British Indian and Javanese Laborers in Suriname* (Gainesville: University Press of Florida, 1998); Lomarsh Roopnarine, "Return Migration of Indentured East Indians from the Caribbean to India, 1838–1920", *Journal of Caribbean History* 40, no. 2 (2006): 308–24.

Appendix 2

Commencement, Stoppage and Resumption Indentured Emigration from Calcutta to Overseas Colonies, 1838–1883

Years	Mauritius	Demerara	Trinidad	Jamaica	Grenada	St Lucia	St Kitts	Natal
1838								
1842	commenced							
1844								
1845		commenced	commenced	commenced				
1846								
1847								
1848				stopped				
1849		stopped	stopped					
1850								
1851		resumed	resumed					
1852								
1853								
1854								
1855								
1856					commenced			
1857								
1858						commenced		
1859				resumed	stopped			
1860						stopped	commenced	commenced
1861					resumed	resumed	stopped	stopped
1862				stopped	stopped	stopped		
1863								
1864								resumed
1865					resumed			stopped
1866				resumed	stopped			
1867				stopped				
1868				resumed				
1869								
1870					resumed			
1871					stopped			
1872								
1873								
1874								resumed
1875								
1876				stopped				
1877				resumed	resumed			
1878					stopped	resumed		
1879				stopped				stopped
1880								resumed
1881	stopped			resumed		stopped		
1882	resumed			stopped				
1883				resumed				

Appendix 2 (continued)

St Vincent	Nevis	Fiji	Reunion	Cayene	Guadeloupe	Martinque	St Croix	Surnam
			commenced					
commenced								
stopped							commenced	
							stopped	
resumed								
			stopped					
stopped								
resumed								
stopped								
resumed								
stopped								
	commenced			commenced	commenced			commenced
resumed	stopped			stopped		commenced		
stopped								stopped
						stopped		
								resumed
		commenced						
resumed		stopped						
stopped								
		resumed						

Sources: Tabulated from various primary and secondary sources. See House of Commons, *Parliamentary Papers* 1910, 1914; House of Commons, *Parliamentary Papers, The General Report of the Colonial Land and Emigration Commissioners* (London: HMSO, 1854–1870); IOR, *India Emigration Proceedings,* 1885; Roberts and Byrne, "Summary Statistics"; Laurence, *Question of Labor;* Look Lai, *Indentured Labor, Caribbean Sugar;* Shepherd, *Transients to Settlers;* Vertovec, *Hindu Trinidad;* Hoefte, *In Place of Slavery;* Roopnarine, "Return Migration".

Appendix 3

Number of East Indian Emigrants Who Were Repatriated Yearly from Jamaica, 1853–1890

Year	Men	Women	Children	Number
1853	-	–	–	1,167
1854	–	–	–	880
1858	–	–	–	126
1871	464	215	248	925
1872	235	81	104	420
1875	269	65	22	356
1876	182	43	26	251
1877	212	62	42	316
1878	167	43	17	237
1879	196	123	97	416
1880	236	91	49	376
1881	219	96	88	403
1882	235	121	92	418
1883	226	113	76	415
1884	41	25	12	78
1885	248	134	89	471
1886	75	45	41	161
1888	279	157	117	553
1890	298	158	111	567
Total				8,066

Source: D.W.D. Comins, *Notes on Emigration from India to Jamaica* (Calcutta: Bengal Secretariat, 1893), 21.

Appendix 4

Number of East Indian Emigrants Paying for Passage from British Guiana to India

Year	Men	Women	Boys	Girls	Total
1862	71	14	–	2	87
1864	89	9	–	3	51
1865	16	12	–	–	28
1867	5	9	–	–	14
1876	6	–	–	–	6
1877	17	8	–	1	26
1878	30	8	2	3	43
1879	28	6	1	–	35
1880	9	2	–	–	11
1881	18	4	2	–	24
1882	5	3	2	–	10
1883	66	13	4	2	85
1884	5	–	1	–	6
1885	38	4	1	1	44
1886	29	2	–	1	32
1887	27	4	–	–	31
1888	49	6	3	–	58
1889	5	–	–	–	5
1890	9	8	1	–	13
Total	472	107	17	13	609

Source: D.W.D. Comins, *Notes on Emigration from India to British Guiana* (Calcutta: Bengal Secretariat, 1893), 43.

Appendix 5

Licence to Recruiter of East Indian Emigrants

This is to certify that _____ is hereby licensed to recruit Emigrants Laborers for _____ _____ conformity with the regulations published and to be published from time to time regarding such recruiting. This license is granted from the 1st of _____ inclusive, and upon the express understanding and condition that the said Recruiter is to be under direct control of the district Magistrate, the Emigrant Agent, and Protector of Emigrants, in all matters relating to such recruiting, and that we shall have full power to suspend or withdraw this License, if he shall not conduct himself in the premises to our satisfaction.

Date this _____ day of 18___   Emigration Agent at for Governor_____
Magistrate_____

Descriptive Roll of the Above Recruiter

Name	Father's name	Age	Caste	Zillah	Pergunnah	Village	Remarks

Source: India Office Records, *Bengal Emigration Proceedings*, September 1862, 3.

Appendix 6

Copy of a Certificate of Indenture

This indenture, made on the first day of April in the year 1876, between _____, as proprietor (or attorney, etc), of Plantation _____, in the county of _____, in the colony of British Guiana, of the one or first part, and the several (Indian, Chinese, etc, as the case may be) immigrants whose names are respectively subscribed hereto, of the other or second part, witnesseth as follows:

> That the said employer agree to hire the services of the said several immigrants, and the said several immigrants agree to serve the said Employer as Labourers for the term of _____ years, commencing on the 1st day of April, 1867, subject in all respects to the provisions of the Consolidated Immigration Ordinance

Appendix 7

Certificate of Completion of Ten Years' Residence

Issued under section 10 of Law _____ of 1891.

This is to certify that _____ ex ship _____ 18___, an immigrant introduced from _____ on the _____ day of _____ 18___, _____ has completed a residence of ten years in Jamaica.

_____

Protector of Immigrants

Law 23 of 1879.

Appendix 8

Example of Old Immigrant's Ticket

Name of Immigrant . . . .
Number . . . .
Name of the Father . . . .
Name of the Mother . . . .
Age (in letters) . . . . Photograph
Stature (in feet and inches). . . . .

Caste . . . .
Mark . . . .
Native Country . . . .
Number of Vessel by which introduced . . . .

This Immigrants is free to engage himself.
Delivered this _____ 186_
Signed:
Protector of Immigrants.

Source: House of Commons, *Parliamentary Papers*, vol. 7 (4159). *The Twenty-ninth General Report of the Colonial Land and Emigration Commissioners* (London: HMSO, 1869), 127.

Appendix 9

Tabulated Statement Showing the Castes of Immigrants Introduced during Season 1889–1890 to Trinidad

Caste	Numbers	Caste	Numbers
Ohamar	647	Kalwar	11
Muhammadan	355	Rajbhuir	9
Ahir and stgope	276	Sonar	9
Chutress, Takur and Rajput	268	Dhobi	9
Koiri	157	Ghassa	8
Kabar	144	Bhuja	7
Kurni	129	Banspore	7
Bhurr	84	Dom	7
Dosad	76	Halwye	6
Kori	76	Buncah	6
Gwala	69	Jat	6
Masuhar	64	Kumar	5
Passi	58	Bagdi	4
Nonia	53	Bahaleah	5
Gararia	40	Kyesth	4
Lodh	43	Bhukta	4
Mulla	33	Koibucto	4
Brahman and Gosame	32	Khandit	4

Appendix 9 (*continued*)

Caste	Numbers	Caste	Numbers
Bind	31	Bhunia	3
Kewat	30	Turha	3
Lohar	29		2
Bhoocar	28	Kanu	2
Bhunji, Mether, Halkore, Lalbegi	32	Dhunia	3
Kachi	28	Zamindar	2
Teli	22	Nat	2
Baraie	22	Boldar	2
Kumbi	19	Thanu and Tanta	2
Kandu	18	Katick	1
Tatwa	16	Christain	1
Nao, Hajam, Napith	16	Pathurin	1
Dhanak	15	Goriah	1
Gour and Ghor	13	Kol	1
Murai and Mura	12	Tamoli, Kaserwani	2
Dhurkar	11	Sandi, Bostom	2
Malli and Bari	11	Total	3,072

Source: D.W.D. Comins, *Notes on Emigration from India to Trinidad* (Calcutta: Bengal Secretariat, 1893), 37.

Appendix 10

Categories of Emigrants Returning from Trinidad to Calcutta 1865

Categories	Men	Women	Children	Total
Completed 10 years industrial residence	266	59	72	397
Completed 5 years and paid their own passage	55	21	1	77
Poor, Invalids, and Vagrants sent back at the expense of the colony	33	7	0	40
Total	354	87	73	514

Source: House of Commons, *Parliamentary Papers,* Vol. 17 (3679), *Twenty-sixth General Report of the Colonial Land and Emigration Commissioners* (London: HMSO, 1866), 29.

Appendix 11

Number of Deaths on the Outward Voyage during the Season 1860–1861

Colony	Number of Ships	Number Embarked	Number of Deaths	Mortality per cent
British Guiana	8	3,152	128	4.0
Trinidad	5	2,023	71	3.4
Jamaica	3	1,057	131	12.3
St Vincent	1	308	10	3.2
Grenada	2	802	22	2.7
St Lucia	1	336	17	5.0

Source: House of Commons, *Parliamentary Papers, Twenty-second General Report of the Colonial Land and Emigration Commissioners* (London: HMSO, 1862), 49.

Notes

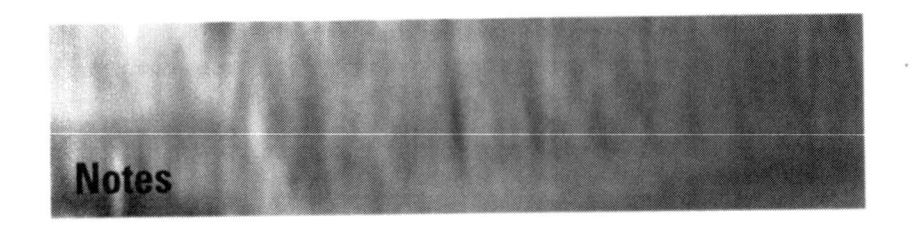

Introduction

1. On history and indenture, see Clem Seecharan, *Sweetening "Bitter Sugar": Jock Campbell, The Booker Reformer in British Guiana, 1934–66* (Kingston: Ian Randle, 2004); Clem Seecharan, "The Shaping of the Indo-Caribbean People in the 1940s", *Journal of Caribbean Studies* 14, no. 2 (2000): 61–92; Clem Seecharan, *Bechu: "Bound Coolie" Radical in British Guiana, 1894–1901* (Kingston: University of the West Indies Press, 1999); Clem Seecharan, *Tiger in the Stars: The Anatomy of Indian Achievement in British Guiana 1919–1929*, Warwick University Caribbean Studies (London: Macmillian, 1997); Clem Seecharan, *India and the Shaping of Indo-Guyanese Imagination, 1890s–1920s* (Leeds: Peepal Tree Press, 1993); Lakshmi Mansingh and Ajai Mansingh, *Home Away from Home: 150 Years of Indian Presence in Jamaica 1845–1995* (Kingston: Ian Randle, 2000); Ron Ramdin, *Arising from Bondage: A History of Indo-Caribbean People* (New York: New York University Press, 2000); Madhavi Kale, *Fragments of Empire: Capital, Slavery, and Indian Indentured Labor Migration in the British West Indies* (Philadelphia: University of Pennsylvania Press, 1998); Keith Laurence, *A Question of Labor: Indentured Immigration into Trinidad and British Guiana, 1875–1917* (New York: St Martin's Press, 1994); Marianne Ramesar, *Survivors of Another Crossing: A History of East Indians in Trinidad, 1880–1946* (St Augustine, Trinidad: University of West Indies Press, 1994); Walton Look Lai, *Indentured Labor, Caribbean Sugar: Chinese and Indian Migrants to the British West Indies, 1838–1917* (Baltimore: Johns Hopkins University Press, 1993); Basdeo Mangru, *A History of East Indian Resistance on the Guyana Sugar Estates, 1869–1948* (New York: Mellon, 1996); Basdeo Mangru,

Benevolent Neutrality: Indian Government Policy and Labor Migration to British Guiana, 1854–1884 (London: Hansib, 1987); Kelvin Singh, *Bloodstained Tombs: The Muharram Massacre, 1884* (London and Basingstoke: Macmillan, 1988); Kusha Haraksingh, "Control and Resistance among Indian Workers: A Study of Labour on the Sugar Plantations of Trinidad, 1875–1917", in *India in the Caribbean*, ed David Dabydeen and Brinsley Samaroo (London: Hansib/University of Warwick, 1987), 61–80; Bridget Brereton, "The Experience of Indentureship: 1845–1917", in *Calcutta to Caroni: The East Indians in Trinidad*, ed. John G. La Guerre (London: Longman, 1974), 26–39; Hugh Tinker, *A New System of Slavery: The Export of Indian Labour Overseas, 1830–1920* (Oxford: Institute of Race Relations, London, 1974); Judith Weller, *The East Indian Indenture in Trinidad* (Rio Piedras, Puerto Rico: Institute of Caribbean Studies, 1968); and E.A. Luckhoo, "The East Indians in British Guiana: From Their Advent to This Colony, to the Present time; A Survey of the Economic, Educational, and Political Aspects", *Timehri: Being the Journal of Royal Agricultural and Commercial Society of British Guiana*, 3rd ser., 6, no. 23 (1919): 53–65. On culture, see Steve Vertovec, *Hindu Trinidad: Religion, Ethnicity and Socio-Economic Change* (London: Macmillan, 1992); Joseph Nevadomsky, "Changes Over Time and Space in the East Indian Family in Rural Trinidad", *Journal of Comparative Family Studies* 11, no. 4 (1980): 434–36; Leo A. Despres, *Cultural Pluralism and Nationalist Politics in British Guiana* (Chicago: Rand McNally, 1967); Johan Speckmann, *Marriage and Kinship among Indians in Suriname* (Assen: Van Gorcum, 1965); Raymond Smith, *British Guiana* (London: Oxford University Press, 1962); Morton Klass, *East Indians in Trinidad: A Study of Cultural Persistence* (New York: Columbia University Press, 1961); and Arthur Niehoff and Jaunita Niehoff, *East Indians in the West Indies*, Milwaukee Public Museum, Publication in Anthropology, no. 6 (Milwaukee: Milwaukee Public Museum, 1960). On politics, see Yogendra K. Malik, *East Indians in Trinidad* (London: Oxford University Press, 1971). On gender, see Verene Shepherd, *Maharani's Misery: Narratives of a Passage from India* (Kingston: University of the West Indies Press, 2002); Verene Shepherd, *Transients to Settlers: The Experience of Indians in Jamaica, 1845–1950* (Leeds: Peepal Tree Press, 1994); Rosanne Kanhai, ed., *Matikor: The Politics of Identity for Indo-Caribbean Women* (St Augustine, Trinidad: University of the West Indies, School of Continuing Studies, 1999); Rosemarijin Hoefte, *In Place of Slavery: A Social History of British Indian and Javanese Laborers in Suriname* (Gainesville: University Press of Florida, 1998); Patricia Mohammed, "The 'Creolization' of Indian Women in Trinidad", in *The Independence Experience, 1962–1987*, ed. Selwyn Ryan (St Augustine, Trinidad: University of the West Indies, 1988), 381–97; Pieter Emmer, "The Great Escape: The Migration of Female Indentured Servants from British India to Surinam, 1873–1916", in *Abolition and Its Aftermath*, ed. P.D. Richardson (London: Frank Cass, 1986), 245–66; and Rhoda Reddock, "Freedom Denied! Indian Women and Indentureship in Trinidad and Tobago, 1854–1917", *Economic and Political Weekly* 20, no. 43 (1985): 79–87. On education, see M.K. Bacchus,

Education and Socio-Cultural Integration in a Plural Society, Occasional Paper Series, no. 6 (Montreal: Centre for Developing Area Studies, McGill University, 1970). On ethnicity, see David Dabydeen and Brinsley Samaroo, eds., *Across Dark Waters: Ethnicity and Indian Identity in the Caribbean* (London: Macmillan, 1996) and *India in the Caribbean* (London: Hansib, 1987). On religion, see Brinsley Samaroo, "In Sick Longing for the Further Shore: Return Migration by Caribbean East Indians During the Nineteenth and Twentieth Centuries", in *Return Migration and Remittances: Developing a Caribbean Perspective*, ed. William F. Stiner, Klaus de Albquerque and Roy S. Bryce-Laporte, Research Institute on Immigration and Ethnic Studies Occasional Papers, no. 3 (Washington, DC: Smithsonian Institution, Washington, DC, 1982), 45–72; and Sarah Morton, *John Morton of Trinidad* (Toronto: Westminster, 1916). On caste, see Colin Clarke, "Caste among Hindus in a Town in San Fernando", in *Caste in Overseas Indian Communities*, ed. Barton M. Schwartz (San Francisco: Chandler, 1967), 165–99; Milton Singer, "The Indian Joint Family in Modern Industry", in *Structure and Change in Indian Society*, ed. Milton Singer and Benard S. Cohn (Chicago: Adline, 1968), 432–52; and Chandra Jayawardena, *Conflict and Solidarity in a Guianese Plantation* (London: University of London, Athlone, 1963). On migration, see Lomarsh Roopnarine, "Indo-Caribbean Intra-Island Migration: Not so Marginalized!" *Social and Economic Studies* 54, no. 2 (2005): 106–36; Lomarsh Roopnarine, "Indo-Caribbean Migration from Periphery to Core", *Caribbean Quarterly* 49, no. 3 (2003): 30–60; Mahin Gosine and Dhanpaul Narine, *Sojourners to Settlers: The Indian Immigrants in the Caribbean and the Americas* (New York: Windsor Press, 1999); and Lesily M. Potter, "The Post-Indenture Experience of East Indians in Guyana, 1871–1922", in *Indenture and Exile: The Indo-Caribbean Experience*, ed. Frank Birbalsingh (Toronto: Tsar, 1989), 71–92. On literature, see Brinda Metha, *Diasporic (Dis)locations: Indo-Caribbean Women Writers Negotiate the Kala Pani* (Kingston: University of the West Indies Press, 2004); Frank Birbalsingh, ed., *Jahaji: An Anthology of Indo-Caribbean Fiction* (Toronto: Tsar, 2000); V.S. Naipaul, *Between Father and Son: Family Letters* (New York: Knopf, 2000); and David Dabydeen, *Coolie Odyssey* (London: Hansib, 1988). On music, see Tina K. Ramnarine, *Creating Their Own Space: The Development of an Indian-Caribbean Musical Tradition* (Kingston: University of the West Indies Press, 2001) and Peter Manuel, *East Indian Music in the West Indies: Tan-Singing, Chutney, and the Making of Indo-Caribbean Culture* (Philadelphia: Temple University Press, 2000). On sports, see Frank Birbalsingh, *The Rise of West Indian Cricket: From Colony to Nation* (London: Hansib, 1996); on identity, see Marina Carter and Khal Torabully. *Coolitude: An Anthology of Indian Labor Diaspora* (London: Anthem Press, 2002).

2. Shepherd, *Transients to Settlers*, 13–22.
3. Tinker, *New System of Slavery*.
4. Samaroo, "In Sick Longing", 46–48.
5. See David Chanderbali, "A Guyanese Perspective" (proceedings of the international seminar From Indentureship to Entrepreneurship: East Indians

and the Socio-Economic Transition in the Caribbean, University of the West Indies, St Augustine, Trinidad, 2003).

6. See Seecharan, *Bechu*.

7. David W. Galenson, *White Servitude in Colonial America* (Cambridge: Cambridge University Press, 1981).

8. David Northrup, *Indentured Labour in the Age of Imperialism, 1834–1922* (Cambridge: Cambridge University Press, 1995).

9. Michael L. Bush, *Servitude in Modern Times* (Cambridge: Polity Press, 2000); Dorothy Shineberg, *The People Trade: Pacific Island Laborers and New Caledonia, 1865–1930* (Honolulu: University of Hawaii Press, 1999); Eric Williams, *From Columbus to Castro: A History of the Caribbean, 1492–1969* (New York: Vintage Books, 1984).

10. Peter H. Jenson, *From Serfdom to Fireburn and Strike: A History of Black Labour in the Danish West Indies, 1848–1916* (St Croix, US Virgin Islands: Antilles Press, 1998). See also the *Coolie Journal* (Danish National Archives, Rigstarkivet, Vest Indiske Lokalarkiver, Den Vest Indiske Regering 1863, Reference 3.81.584) for a report on Indian Indenture Service in St Croix. This document is in English.

11. Bush, *Servitude in Modern Times*, 206.

12. PRO (CO), *Report of the Committee from India to the Crown Colonies and Protectorates (Sanderson Committee)*, 1910. vol. 27, Cd. 5192–94, 9.

13. Galenson, *White Servitude in Colonial America*, 182.

14. Immanuel Wallerstein, *The Modern World-System, Capitalist Agriculture and the Origins of the European World-Economy in the Sixteenth Century* (New York: Academic Press, 1974).

15. C. Kondapi, *Indians Overseas, 1838–1949* (New Delhi: India Council of World Affairs, 1951); PRO (CO), *Report by Geoghegan on Immigration from India*, 1874. vol. 47, C. 314.

16. C. James Scott, *Domination and the Arts of Resistance: Hidden Transcript* (New Haven: Yale University Press, 1990).

17. Ibid., 1–16.

18. Reddock, "Freedom Denied!", 79–87.

19. Emmer, "Great Escape", 245–66; Brian Moore, "The Retention of Caste Notions among the Indian Immigrants in British Guiana During the Nineteenth Century", *Comparative Studies in Society and History* 19 (1977): 96–107.

20. See K. Homi Bhabha, *The Location of Culture* (London: Routledge, 1994); Peter Childs and Patrick Williams, *An Introduction to Post-Colonial Theory* (London: Prentice Hall, 1997), 131.

Chapter 1

1. P.H. Parry and Phillip Sherlock, *The Short History of the West Indies* (London: Macmillan, 1982), 201.

2. Williams, *From Columbus to Castro*, 108–9.

3. Donald E. Smith, *India as a Secular State* (Princeton: Princeton University Press, 1963), 337–39.

4. William J. Duiker and Jackson J. Spielvogel, *World History*, 4th ed. (Belmont, Calif.: Thomson and Wadsworth, 2003), 587.

5. Micheal Burawoy, "The Functions and Reproduction of Migrant Labor: Comparative Material from Southern Africa and the United States", *American Journal of Sociology* 8, no. 5 (1976): 1050.

6. Among others, see Laurence, *Question of Labor*, for Trinidad; Mangru, *Benevolent Neutrality*, for Guyana; Hoefte, *In Place of Slavery*, for Suriname; Shepherd, *Transients to Settlers*, for Jamaica; Look Lai, *Indentured Labor, Caribbean Sugar*, for the Caribbean; and Tinker, *New System of Slavery*, for East Indians overseas.

7. Wallerstein, *Modern World-System*.

8. See also Ernest Mandel, "The Laws of Uneven Development", *New Left Review* 59 (1970): 19–40.

9. Gail Omvedt, "Towards a Theory of Colonialism", *Insurgent Sociologist* 3 (1973): 1.

10. Burawoy, "Functions and Reproduction of Migrant Labor", 1050–51.

11. Terry A. Repak, *Working on Washington: Central American Workers in the Nation's Capital* (Philadelphia: Temple University Press, 1995), 8.

12. See also Charles H. Wood, "Equilibrium and Historical-Structural Perspective on Migration", *International Migration Review* 16, no. 2 (1982): 298–319.

13. A. Portes, "Migration and Underdevelopment", *Politics and Society* 8, no. 1 (1978): 11.

14. Lucie Cheng and Edna Bonacich, eds., *Labor Immigration Under Capitalism* (Los Angeles: University of California Press, 1984).

15. Because major emigration of East Indian labour occurred only after the British annexed India, it is implicit that the socioeconomic changes brought about by colonization fostered this process. See S. Mazumdar, "Colonial Impact and Punjabi Emigration to the United States", in *Labor Immigration Under Capitalism: Asian Workers in the United States before World War II*, ed. Lucie Cheng and Edna Bonacich (Los Angeles: University of California Press, 1984), 319.

16. K.S. Sandhu, *Indians in Malaya: Some Aspects of their Immigration and Settlement, 1786–1957* (Cambridge: Cambridge University Press, 1969); Romesh Dutt, *The Economic History of India* (New York: A.M. Kelly, 1969); Kondapi, *Indians Overseas*.

17. Portes, "Migration and Underdevelopment", 1–48.

18. Kondapi, *Indians Overseas*, 1–2; Dutt, *Economic History of India*.

19. Portes, "Migration and Underdevelopment", 24.

20. P. Saha, *Emigration of Indian Labor, 1834–1900* (New Delhi: People's Publishing House, 1970); K. Datta, *Survey of India's Social Life and Economic Conditions in the Eighteenth Century (1707–1813)* (Calcutta: Firma, 1961).

21. Brij V. Lal, *Girmitiyas: The Origins of the Fiji Indians* (Canberra: Journal of Pacific History, 1983); Brij V. Lal, "Fiji Girmitiyas: The Background to Banishment", in *Rama's Banishment*, ed. Vijay Mishra (Auckland: Heineman, 1979), 12–39; Dietmar Rothermund, "Government, Landlord and Tenant in India, 1875–1900", *Indian Economic and Social History Review* 6 (1969): 351–67; Thomas R. Metcalf, *The Aftermath of Revolt, India 1857–1877* (Princeton, NJ: Princeton University Press, 1964).

22. IOR, *Bengal Emigration Proceedings*, November 1862, 25.

23. Mangru, *Benevolent Neutrality*, 61. See also B. Hiejle, "Slavery and Agriculture Bondage in South India in the Nineteenth Century", *Scandinavian Economic History Review* 15, no. 1–2 (1967): 71–126; Daniel Thorner and Alice Thorner, *Land and Labor in India* (Bombay: Asia Publishing House, 1962).

24. Sandhu, *Indians in Malaya*, 41.

25. Eric Wolf, *Peasant Wars in the Twentieth Century* (New York: Harper and Row, 1969), 279.

26. James Henslin, ed., *Essentials of Sociology: A Down to Earth Approach*, 4th ed. (Boston: Allyn and Bacon, 2003), 361.

27. See S. Ambiragan, "Malthusian Population Theory and Indian Famine Policy in the Nineteenth Century", *Population Studies* 30, no. 1 (1976): 5–14.

28. Ibid., 10.

29. K.L. Gillion, *Fiji's Indian Emigrant* (London: Oxford University Press, 1962), 28.

30. Duiker and Spielvogel, *World History*, 45–46.

31. Dale Bisnauth, *The Settlement of Indians in Guyana, 1890–1930* (Leeds: Peepal Tree Press, 2001), Laurence; *Question of Labor*, Roland Lardiniois, "Famine, Epidemics and Mortality in South India: A Reappraisal of the Demographic Crisis of 1876–1878", *Economic and Political Weekly* 20, no. 11 (1985): 454–65; H.S. Srivastava, *The History of Indian Famines and Development of Famine Policy, 1858–1918* (Delhi: Agra, 1967).

32. Commons, *Parliamentary Papers* (1874), vol. 47 (C. 314), 74.

33. J.C. Jha, "The Indian Mutiny-cum-Revolt of 1857 and Trinidad (West Indies)", *Indian Studies: Past and Present* 13, no. 4 (1972): 419–30.

34. PRO (CO), "Hon. Charles T. Cox to C.O.", 8 February 1906,111:554.

35. George A. Grierson, *Report on Colonial Emigration from Bengal Presidency* (Calcutta: Bengal Secretariat, 1883), 21.

36. IOR, *Bengal Emigration Proceedings*, March 1866, 51.

37. IOR, *Bengal Emigration Proceedings*, January 1862, 3.

38. Metcalf, *Aftermath of Revolt*.

39. Commons, *Parliamentary Papers* (1910), vol. 27 (Cd. 5192–94), 8.

40. Quoted in E. Evansohn, "Workers and Imperialism: Where Is the Aristocracy of Labor", *Insurgent Sociologist* 7, no. 2 (1977): 56.

41. IOR, *Bengal Emigration Proceedings* August 1864, 24.
42. PRO (CO), *British Guiana: Emigration*, no. 31 (25 February 1860), 111:326.
43. Portes, "Migration and Underdevelopment", 10.
44. Gillion, *Fiji's Indian Emigrant*, 23.
45. See J. Gallagher and Ronald Robinson, "The Imperialism of Free Trade", *Economic History Review* 6, no. 1 (1953): 1–15.
46. PRO (CO), Agent Mitchell to Colonial Office, 8 February 1906.
47. Gail Omvedt, "Migration in Colonial India: The Articulation of Feudalism and Capitalism by the Colonial State", *Journal of Peasant Studies* 7 (1980): 185–212.
48. PRO (CO), Agent Mitchell to Colonial Office, 9 February 1906, 111:553.
49. See Vertovec, *Hindu Trinidad*; A. L. Basham, *Studies in Indian History and Culture* (Calcutta: Sambodhi, 1964), 162–66.
50. PRO (CO), 25 February 1860.
51. Grierson, *Report on Colonial Emigration*, 19.
52. IOR, *Bengal Emigration Proceedings*, November 1862, 26.
53. In Dwarka Nath, *History of Indians in British Guiana* (London: Nelson, 1975), 82.
54. IOR, *Census of India* (London, 1921), vol. 1, part 1, 83 and 136–51.
55. Joanna Liddle and Rama Joshi, *Daughters of Independence: Gender, Caste, and Class in India* (New Brunswick, NJ: Rutgers University Press, 1986), 25.
56. IOR, *Bengal Emigration Proceedings*, April 1862, 15.
57. H.H. Risely, *The Tribes and Castes of Bengal* (Calcutta: Bengal Secretariat Press, 1892), 2:139.
58. Usha Deka, "Early Instances of Race-Crossing in India", *Man in India* 43, no. 4 (1954): 275.
59. Risely, *Tribes and Castes of Bengal*, 2:233.
60. IOR, *Bengal Hurkura*, 21 December 1838.
61. Ramdin, *Arising From Bondage*, 26.
62. IOR, *Bengal Emigration Proceedings*, June 1865, 5.
63. PRO (CO), 9 February 1906.
64. See K.L. Gillion, "The Sources of Indian Emigration to Fiji", *Population Studies* 10 (1956): 151
65. Laurence, *Question of Labor*, 105.
66. PRO (CO), Government Emigration for Trinidad to Colonial Office, 15 August 1904, 294:430.
67. Ibid.
68. Gillion, *Fiji's Indian Emigrant*, 48–49.
69. Prabhu P. Mohapatra, "Restoring the Family: Wife Murders and the Making of a Sexual Contract for Indian Immigrant Labor in the British Caribbean Colonies, 1860–1920", *Studies in History* 11, no. 2 (1995): 231.

70. Raymond Smith, "Some Characteristics of Indian Immigrants to British Guiana", *Population Studies* 13, no. 1 (1959): 34–39.

71. See H.V.P. Bronkhurst, *The Colony British Guiana and its Labouring Population* (London: T. Woolmer, 1883), 281–99.

72. Vertovec, *Hindu Trinidad*, 93.

73. Tinker, *A New System of Slavery*, 51; see also Look Lai, *Indentured Labor, Caribbean Sugar*.

74. IOR, *Bengal Emigration Proceedings*, November 1862, 4.

75. IOR, *Bengal Hurkaru*, 4 July 1838.

76. Ibid., 15 July 1838.

77. IOR, *India Emigration Proceedings*, 26 August 1871, 39–40.

78. C.F. Andrews, "India's Emigration Problem", *Foreign Affairs* 8, no. 3 (1930): 433.

79. Sandhu, *Indians in Malaya*, 32.

80. See I.M. Cumpston, "Survey of Indian Immigration to British Tropical Colonies to 1910", *Population Studies* 10, no. 2 (1956): 158–65.

81. Commons, *Parliamentary Papers* (1910), vol. 27 (Cd. 5192–94), 10.

82. IOR, *Bengal Emigration Proceedings*, March 1866, 51.

83. IOR, *India Emigration Proceedings*, 26 August 1871, 39–40.

84. See Frantz Fanon, *The Wretched of the Earth* (New York: Grove Press, 1968).

85. Laurence, *Question of Labor*.

86. IOR, *India Emigration Proceedings*, September 1871, 60.

87. See Liddle and Joshi, "Gender and Imperialism", 72–78.

88. E.M. Petras, "Towards a Theory of International Labor: The New Division of Labor", in *Sourcebook on the New Immigration*, ed. Roy Bryce-Laporte (Washington, DC: Smithsonian Institution, Research Institute on Immigration and Ethnic Studies, 1979), 434–49.

Chapter 2

1. See Antonio Gramsci, *Selections from the Prison Notebooks*, ed. and trans. Quinten Hoare and Geoffrey Nowell Smith (London: Wishart, 1971).

2. See Michael Foucault, *The Archaeology of Knowledge*, trans. A.M. Sheridan Smith (New York: Pantheon Books, 1972).

3. Edward Said, *Orientalism* (Harmondsworth: Penguin, 1978), 32.

4. Ibid., 207.

5. Gramsci, *Selections from the Prison Notebooks*.

6. Susan Bayly, *The New Cambridge History of India*, vol. 3: *Caste, Society, and Politics in India from the Eighteenth Century to the Modern Age* (Cambridge: Cambridge University Press, 1999), 100.

7. Edward Said, *The World, the Text and the Critic* (London: Faber and Faber, 1984), 232; Roland Inden, *Imagining India* (Oxford: Basil Blackwell, 1990), 36.

8. Inden, *Imagining India*, 8.

9. Tinker, *New System of Slavery*.

10. Haraksingh, "Control and Resistance", 63.

11. See Franklin Knight, *The Caribbean: The Genesis of a Fragmented Nationalism* (New York: Oxford University Press, 1990); Brain Moore, *Race, Power and Social Segmentation in Colonial Society: Guyana After Slavery 1838-1891* (New York: Gordon and Breach, 1987); William Green, *British Slave Emancipation: The Sugar Colonies and the Great Experiment, 1830-1865* (Oxford: Clarendon, 1976); David Lowenthal, *West Indian Societies* (New York: Oxford University Press, 1972); Orlando Patterson, *The Sociology of Slavery* (London: MacGibbon and Kee, 1967); Elsa Goveia, *Slave Society in the British Leeward Islands at the end of the Eighteenth Century* (New Haven: Yale University Press, 1965); L.J. Ragatz, *The Fall of the Planter Class in the British Caribbean, 1763-1833* (New York: Octagon, 1971); Charles Wagely, "Plantation America: A Culture Sphere", in *Caribbean Studies: A Symposium*, ed. Vera Rubin (Seattle: University of Washington Press, 1960), 1-13.

12. Knight, *The Caribbean*, 124; Moore, *Race, Power and Social Segmentation*, 5-7; Green, *British Slave Emancipation*, 33.

13. Eric Wolf and Sidney Mintz, "Haciendas and Plantations in Middle America and the Antilles", *Social and Economic Studies* 6, no. 3 (1957): 380-412.

14. Lowenthal, *West Indian Societies*, 50.

15. Nigel Bolland, "Systems of Dominations after Slavery: The Control of Land and Labor in British West Indies after 1838", *Comparative Studies in Society and History* 23, no. 4 (1981): 594.

16. Walter Rodney, *How Europe Underdeveloped Africa* (Washington, DC: Howard University Press, 1981).

17. Fernando Henriques, *Family and Colour in Jamaica* (London: MacGibbon and Kee, 1953).

18. Scott, *Domination and the Arts of Resistance*.

19. See George Eliot, *Adam Bede* (1859; reprint, Harmondsworth: Penguin, 1981).

20. Scott, *Domination and the Arts of Resistance*, 3.

21. Ibid., 10.

22. Tetsuo Najita and Irwin Scheiner, *Japanese Thought in the Tokugawa Period, 1600-1868: Methods and Metaphors* (Chicago: University of Chicago Press, 1978); Dev Raj Channa, *Slavery in Ancient India* (New Delhi: People's Publishing House, 1960); Orlando Patterson, *Slavery and Social Death: A Comparative Study* (Cambridge: Harvard University Press, 1982).

23. Karl Marx and Friedrich Engels, *The Communist Manifesto* (1848; reprint, Harmondsworth: England, 1967), 80.

24. Singh, *Bloodstained Tombs*; see also Honoré de Balzac, *A Harlot High and Low*, trans. Reyner Happenstall (Harmondsworth: Penguin, 1970).

25. Scott, *Domination and the Arts of Resistance*, 27.

26. Theodore Rosengarten, *All God's Danger: The Life of Nate Shaw* (New York: Knopf, 1974), 591.
27. Ibid.
28. Richard Hoggart, *The Use of Literacy: Aspects of the Working Class life* (London: Chatto and Windus, 1954), 77–78; Scott, *Domination and the Arts of Resistance*, 74.
29. Patterson, *Sociology of Slavery*, 11.
30. R.S. Khare, *The Untouchable as Himself: Ideology, Identity, and Pragmatism among the Lucknow Chamars* (Cambridge Studies in Cultural Systems, no. 8, Cambridge: Cambridge University Press, 1984), 124.
31. Michel Foucault, *The History of Sexuality: An Introduction*, trans. R. Hurley (New York: Vintage Books, 1980), 1:95.
32. C. James Scott, *Weapons of the Weak: Everyday Forms of Peasant Resistance* (New Haven: Yale University Press, 1985), 28–47.
33. Eric Hobsbawn, "Peasants and Politics", *Journal of Peasant Studies* 1, no. 1 (1973): 3–22.
34. Tyran Ramnarine, "Over a Hundred Years of East Indian Disturbances on the Sugar Estates of Guyana 1869–1978: An Historical Overview", in *India in the Caribbean*, ed. David Dabydeen and Brinsley Samaroo (London: Hansib/ University of Warwick, 1987), 119–44; Mangru, *History of East Indian Resistance*; Haraksingh, "Control and Resistance".
35. IOR, *India Emigration Proceedings*, 1874, 97.
36. Singh, *Bloodstained Tombs*, 61–69; Ramnarine, "Over a Hundred Years", 173.
37. Moore, *Race, Power and Social Segmentation*, 173.
38. Noorkumar Mahabir, *The Still Cry: Personal Accounts of East Indians in Trinidad and Tobago during Indentureship (1845–1917)* (Ithaca, NY: Calaloux, 1985), 112.
39. Michael Adas, *Prophets of Rebellion: Millenarian Protest against European Colonial Order* (Chapel Hill: University of North Carolina Press, 1979), 217–47.
40. Barrington Moore, Jr., *Injustice: The Social Bases of Obedience and Revolt* (White Plains, NY: M.E. Sharpe, 1987), 80–84.
41. Sharon S. Brehm and Jack W. Brehm, *Psychological Reactance. A Theory of Freedom and Control* (New York: Academic Press, 1981), 4.
42. D.W.D. Comins, *Notes on Emigration from India to British Guiana* (Calcutta: Bengal Secretariat, 1893), 38.
43. Rosamunde A. Renard, "Labour Relations in Post-Slavery Martinique and Guadeloupe 1858–1870", in *Caribbean Freedom: Economy and Society from Emancipation to the Present*, ed. Hilary Beckles and Verene Shepherd (Kingston: Ian Randle, 1996), 165–66.
44. Shepherd, *Transients to Settlers*, 70.
45. Moore, *Race, Power and Social Segmentation*; Alan H. Adamson, *Sugar Without Slaves: The Political History of British Guiana, 1834–1904* (New Haven: Yale University Press, 1972).

46. Sidney Mintz, "The Origins of Reconstituted Peasantries", in *Caribbean Transformation*, ed. Sidney Mintz (Baltimore: Johns Hopkins University Press, 1974), 146–56.
47. Moore, *Race, Power and Social Segmentation*, 172.
48. Look Lai, *Indentured Labor, Caribbean Sugar*, 148–53.
49. Renard, "Labour Relations in Post-Slavery Martinique", 165.
50. In Niehoff and Niehoff, *East Indians*, 19.
51. Laurence, *Question of Labor*, 491.
52. IOR, *India Emigration Proceedings*, 1878, 54
53. Ibid. 1874, 2.
54. Ibid., appendix 4.
55. Mangru, *Benevolent Neutrality*, 69.
56. Haraksingh, "Control and Resistance", 68.
57. In Scott, *Weapons of the Weak*, 246.
58. Emile Durkheim, *The Division of Labour in Society* (New York: Free Press, 1964).
59. Laurence Levine, *Black Culture and Black Consciousness: Afro-American Folk Thought from Slavery to Freedom* (Oxford: Oxford University Press, 1977), 346–47.
60. Ibid., 358.
61. Derek Walcott, "The Antilles: Fragments of Epic Memory", Nobel Lecture (http://nobelprize.org/literature/laureates/1992/walcott-lecture.html). It is coincidental that I am writing about *Holi* or *Phagwa* in the first week of March; a Hindu festival/celebration that survived the wrath of indentured servitude. The festival of *Holi* is celebrated on the day after the full moon in early March every year. Initially, it was a festival to celebrate good harvests and fertility of the land. *Holi* is now a symbolic commemoration of a legend from Hindu mythology. The story revolves around a king who resents his son Prahlada for worshipping Lord Vishnu. He attempts to kill his son but fails each time. Finally, the king's sister Holika, who is said to be immune to burning, sits with the boy in a huge fire. However, the Prince Prahlada emerges unscathed, while his aunt burns to death. *Holi* is a festival that expresses the eventual triumph of faith in God. *Holi* is spread over sixteen days throughout the Hindu Caribbean.
62. Hobsbawn, "Peasants and Politics", 13.
63. Scott, *Domination and the Arts of Resistance*, 158.
64. Singh, *Bloodstained*, 6–7; see also Frank Korom, *Hosay Trinidad* (Philadelphia: University of Pennsylvania Press, 2002).
65. Chandra Jayawardena, "Ideology and Conflict in Lower Class Communities", *Comparative Studies in Society and History* 10 (1968): 413–46.
66. Seecharan, *Bechu*.
67. Jayawardena, "Ideology and Conflict", 440–41.
68. Walcott, "The Antilles".
69. Scott, *Weapons of the Weak*, 282.
70. Roy Heath, *The Shadow Bride* (New York: Persa Books, 1996), 4.
71. Sigmund Freud, "Humor", *Inter-journal of Psycho-Analysis* 9 (1928): 1–6.

72. Ibid., 3.
73. Ibid., 3–6.
74. Ibid.
75. Lomarsh Roopnarine, "Creating Opportunities out of Indo-Caribbean Indenture" (paper presented at the conference on Globalization, Diaspora and Identity Formation, Paramaribo, Suriname, February 2004).
76. See Ron Jenkins, *Subversive Laughter: The Liberating Power of Comedy* (Toronto: The Free Press, 1994).
77. John J. Macionis, *Sociology*, 10th ed. (Upper Saddle River, NJ: Prentice Hall, 2005), 157.
78. Freud, "Humor", 3–6; John Morreall, ed. *The Philosophy of Laughter and Humor* (Albany: State University of New York Press, 1987), 111; Soren Kierkegaard, *Concluding Unscientific Postscript*, trans. David Swenson and Walter Lowrie (Princeton: Princeton University Press, 1941).
79. Morreall, *Philosophy of Laughter*, 131.
80. Kenneth Burke, *Attitudes Toward History* (Los Altos, Calif.: Hermes, 1984), 43.

Chapter 3

1. Harry Elmer Barnes, *The History of Western Civilization*, vol. 1 (New York: Harcourt, Brace, 1935); Lewis Henry Morgan, *Ancient Society* (1877; reprint, Tucson: University of Arizona Press, 1985); Gerhard and Jean Lenski, *Human Societies: An Introduction to Macrosociology*, 5th ed. (New York: McGraw-Hill, 1987).
2. Larry Naylor, *Culture and Change: An Introduction* (Westport, Conn.: Bergin and Garvey, 1996).
3. Joseph Nevadomsky, "Changes in Hindu Institutions in an Alien Environment", *Eastern Anthropologist* 33, no. 1 (1980): 40.
4. Franklin Frazier, *The Negro Family in the United States* (Chicago: University of Chicago Press, 1939).
5. Melville Herskovits, *The Myth of the Negro Past* (New York: Harpers, 1941).
6. M.G. Smith, *The Plural Society in the British West Indies* (Berkeley: University of California Press, 1965); see also J.S. Furnivall, *Colonial Policy and Practice: A Comparative Study of Burma and Netherlands India* (Cambridge: Cambridge University Press, 1948).
7. Raymond Smith, *British Guiana*; Lloyd Braithwaite, "Social Stratification and Cultural Pluralism", *Annals of the New York Academy of Sciences* 83 (1960): 816–31.
8. See Ralph Premdas, "Diversity and Liberation in the Caribbean: The Decentralist Policy Challenge in the New Millennium", in *Contending with Destiny: The Caribbean in the Twenty-first Century*, ed. Kenneth Hall and Denis Benn, 161–78 (Kingston: Ian Randle, 2000); Mohammed, "'Creolization' of Indian Women in Trinidad"; Lomarsh Roopnarine, "Indo-Caribbean Social Identity", *Caribbean Quarterly* 52, no. 1 (2006): 1–11.

9. Bacchus, *Education*.

10. Nevadomsky, "Changes Over Time and Space", 434–36; Carole Yawney, "Drinking Patterns and Alcoholism in Trinidad", in *McGill Studies in Caribbean Anthropology*, ed. F. Henry (Montreal: McGill University, 1969), 34–48

11. Jayawardena, *Conflict and Solidarity*.

12. Steve Vertevoc, *The Hindu Diaspora: Comparative Patterns* (London: Routledge, 2000); Lowenthal, *West Indian Societies*.

13. Leo Davids, "The East Indian Family Overseas", *Social and Economic Studies* 13 (1964): 383–96; Niehoff and Niehoff, *East Indians*; Klass, *East Indians in Trinidad*; Smith, *British Guiana*; Leo A. Despres, "Anthropology, Cultural Pluralism and the Study of Complex Societies", *Cultural Anthropology* 9, no. 1 (1968): 3–26; Despres, *Cultural Pluralism*; Malik, *East Indians in Trinidad*.

14. Klass, *East Indians in Trinidad*, 230–49.

15. Niehoff and Niehoff, *East Indians*, 101.

16. Despres, *Cultural Pluralism*; Smith, *British Guiana*.

17. Daniel Crowley, "Cultural Assimilation in a Multiracial Society", *Annals of the New York Academy of Sciences* 83 (1960): 850–54; Daniel Crowley, "Plural and Differential Acculturation in Trinidad", *American Anthropologist* 57 (1957): 817–24.

18. See Burton Benedict, "Caste in Mauritius", in *Caste in Overseas Indian Communities*, ed. Barton M. Schwartz (San Francisco: Chandler, 1967): 21–42.

19. Emile Senart, *Caste in India: Facts and the System*, trans. Sir E. Denison Ross (London: Methuen, 1930), 94.

20. Ralph W. Nicholas, "Structures of Politics in the Indian Villages of Southern Asia", in *Structure and Change in Indian Society*, ed. Milton Singer and Bernard S. Cohen (Chicago: Aldine, 1968), 243–63.

21. Brereton, "Experience of Indentureship", 26.

22. Smith, "Some Characteristics", 34–39.

23. Renard, "Labour Relations in Post-Slavery Martinique".

24. Clarke, "Caste among Hindus", 177.

25. Laurence, *Question of Labor*, 233.

26. In Speckmann, *Marriage and Kinship*, 105.

27. J.H. Hutton, *Caste in India* (London: Oxford University Press, 1951), 87.

28. Bronkhurst, *Colony of British Guiana*, 285; Moore, "Retention of Caste Notions", 103.

29. D.W.D. Comins, *Notes on Emigration from India to Trinidad* (Calcutta: Bengal Secretariat, 1893), 37.

30. Ibid., 8.

31. H.S. Morris, "Caste among Indians of Uganda", in *Caste in Overseas Indian Communities*, ed. Barton M. Schwartz (San Francisco: Chandler, 1967), 276.

32. Ibid.

33. Mahabir. *The Still Cry*, 102–3.

34. Jayawardena, *Conflict and Solidarity*, 18.

35. Seecharan, *Bechu*, 25.

36. Walter Rodney, *A History of Guyanese Working People, 1881–1904* (Baltimore: Johns Hopkins University Press, 1981),156.

37. Morton, *John Morton*, 70.

38. Mangru, *Benevolent Neutrality*, 182.

39. Peter Van der Veer and Steve Vertevoc, "Brahmanism Abroad: On Caribbean Hinduism an as Ethnic Religion", *Ethnology* 30 (1991): 151; Hoefte, *In Place of Slavery*, 166–67.

40. Mahabir, *The Still Cry*, 98.

41. Prakash Vatuk, "Protest Songs of East Indians in British Guiana", *Journal of American Folklore* 77, no. 305 (1964): 230–31.

42. Kelvin Singh, "East Indians and the Larger Society", in *Calcutta to Caroni: The East Indians in Trinidad*, ed. John G. La Guerre (London: Longman, 1974), 49.

43. Ibid., 49.

44. Pauline Mahar Kolenda , "Region, Caste and Family Structure: A Comparative Study of the Indian 'Joint' Family", in *Structure and Change in Indian Society*, ed Milton Singer and Benard S. Cohn (Chicago: Adline, 1968), 339–96.

45. David Mandelbaum, *Society in India* (Berkeley and Los Angeles: University of California Press, 1970), 36.

46. Singer, "Indian Joint Family", 426.

47. See Frederick G. Bailey, "The Joint Family in India: A Framework for Discussion", *Economic Weekly* 12 (1960): 345–52; I.P. Desai, "The Joint Family in India: An Analysis", *Sociological Bulletin* 5 (1956): 144–56; Savitri Shahani, "The Joint Family: A Case Study", *Economic Weekly* 13 (1961): 1823–28.

48. Mandelbaum, *Society in India*, 36–37; Davids, "East Indian Family Overseas", 391.

49. Seecharan, "Shaping of the Indo-Caribbean People", 62–63.

50. Klass, *East Indians in Trinidad*, 104.

51. Mandelbaum, *Society in India*, 60.

52. Ibid., 36.

53. Ibid., 91.

54. Usharbudh Arya, *Ritual Songs and Folksongs of the Hindus Of Surinam* (Leiden: E.J. Brill, 1968), 135.

55. Smith and Jayawardena, "Marriage and Family amongst East Indians in British Guiana", *Social and Economic Studies* 8, no. 4 (1959): 336.

56. For an explanation of these philosophies see Jawaharlal Nehru, *The Discovery of India* (Oxford: Oxford University Press, 1989), 183–92.

Chapter 4

1. A.S. Altekar, *The Position of Women in Hindu Civilization* (Delhi: Motilal Banarsidass, 1962), 359.

2. Basham, *Studies in Indian History and Culture*, 21; see also Kamala Basham, *The Wonder That India Was* (New York: Traplinger, 1968), 180–81; Kamala Bhasin, *The Position of Women in India* (Bombay: Leslie Sawhany Programme of Training for Democracy, 1973).

3. Nehru, *Discovery of India*, 315; Liddle and Joshi, *Daughters of Independence*, 64.

4. Ibid., 27.

5. Maitrayee Mukhopadhyay, *Silver Shackles: Women and Development in India* (Oxford: Oxfam, 1984), 23–24.

6. C. Clementi-Ojha, "Outside the Norms: Women Ascetics in Hindu Society", *Economic and Political Weekly* 23, no. 18 (1988): 34–36.

7. In Geraldine Forbes, *Women in India* (Cambridge: Cambridge University Press, 1996), 13.

8. Ibid., 19.

9. Liddle and Joshi, *Daughters of Independence*, 26.

10. Verene Shepherd, *Women in Caribbean History* (Kingston: Ian Randle, 1999); Madhavi Kale, "Projecting Identities: Empire and Indentured Labor Migration from India to Trinidad and British Guiana, 1836–1885", in *Nation and Migration*, ed. Peter van der Veer (Philadelphia: University of Pennsylvania Press, 1995), 73–92; Kale, *Fragments of Empire*; Mohapatra, "Restoring the Family"; Laurence *Question of Labor*; Mangru, *Benevolent Neutrality*; Hoefte, *In Place of Slavery*; Reddock, "Freedom Denied", 79–87; E.L. Erickerson, "Introduction of East Indian Coolies into the British West Indies", *Journal of Modern History* 6 (1934): 127–46.

11. Shepherd, *Maharani's Misery*; Shepherd, *Women in Caribbean History*; Hoefte, *In Place of Slavery*; Laurence, *Question of Labor*; Look Lai, *Indentured Labour, Caribbean Sugar*; Mangru, *Benevolent Neutrality*; Reddock, "Freedom Denied".

12. Remarkably, the East Indian population in the Caribbean was almost equal in gender ratio when the indenture system ended in 1917. In British Guiana and in Trinidad, for example, the female–male ratio rose to 73:100 in 1891 and 61:100 in 1900, respectively. Shepherd found a similar trend in all the East Indian Caribbean territories and stated that by the 1960s the female–male ratio among the Caribbean East Indian population was equal. Several factors explain this change: a greater mortality among men under indenture, women retreating from the plantations and taking up domestic roles, and a natural increase in the population mainly due to the improvement of working and living conditions (*Women in Caribbean History*, 120). See Lomarsh Roopnarine, "Indo-Guyanese Migration: From Plantation to Metropolis", *Immigrants and Minorities* 20, no. 2 (2001): 1–25; Erickerson, "Introduction of East Indian Coolies".

13. Roopnarine, *Immigrants and Minorities*, 1–25.

14. Knight, *The Caribbean*, 132; B.W. Higman, *Slave Population and Economy in Jamaica, 1807–1834* (Cambridge: Cambridge University Press, 1976).

15. Forbes, *Women*, 176–77.

16. IOR, *Bengal Emigration Proceedings*, October 1860, 3.
17. PRO (CO), R.W.S. Mitchell to R. Mcleod, 15 April 1891, 384:182, no. 3046.
18. Reddock, "Freedom Denied".
19. Comins, *Notes on Emigration from India to British Guiana*, 7.
20. Joann Lublin, "Women at Top are Distant from CEO Jobs", *Wall Street Journal*, 28 February 1996, B1.
21. PRO (CO), Note by Mr. C.W. Doorly, on the Methods of Recruiting Emigrants in the Madras Presidency to Colonial Secretary, 30 October 1915, 571:3.
22. Ibid.
23. James McNeill and Chimman Lal, *Report to the Government of India on the Conditions of Indian Immigrants in Four British Colonies and Suriname*, Part 1, *Trinidad and British Guiana* (London: HMSO, 1915), 314.
24. Jeremy Poynting, "East Indian Women in the Caribbean: Experience and Voice", in *India in the Caribbean*, ed. David Dabydeen and Brinsley Samaroo (London: Hansib, 1987), 231; Donald Wood, *Trinidad in Trinidad* (London: Oxford University Press, 1968).
25. Mohapatra, "Restoring the Family", 232.
26. See Bronkhurst, *Among the Hindus*; Laurence, *Question of Labor*, 280.
27. IOR, *India Emigration Proceedings*, Statistics of Women-Murder in India, September 1872, 333.
28. Walter C. Reckless, *The Crime Problem*, 5th ed. (New York: Appleton, 1973).
29. Gresham M. Sykes and David Matza, "Techniques of Neutralization", in *Down to Earth Sociology: Introductory Readings*, 5th ed., ed. James Henslin (New York: Free Press, 1988), 225–31.
30. See Henslin, *Essentials of Sociology*.
31. See Shepherd, *Maharani's Misery*.
32. bell hooks, *Yearning: Race, Gender, and Cultural Politics* (Boston: South End Press, 1990); M. Seenarine, *Indentured Indian Women in Colonial Guyana: Recruitment, Migration, Labor and Caste* (http://saxakali.com/indocarib/sojourner3.htm, 1999).
33. L.H.C. Phillips, "Single Men in Barracks: Some Memories of Plantation Life", *Timehri: Being the Journal of Royal Agricultural and Commercial Society of British Guiana*, 4th ser., 40 (1961): 32.
34. Shepherd, *Maharani's Misery*, 77.
35. Poynting, "East Indian Women", 234.
36. Mangru, *Benevolent Neutrality*, 225; see also Tinker, *New System of Slavery*, 203; Morton, *John Morton*, 343; Weller, *East Indian Indenture in Trinidad*, 71–72. The selling of daughters was related to two of eight forms of marriage that were/ are practised in India. It was either an *Asura*, marriage by purchase, or a *Davia*, a marriage where someone gives a daughter to a sacrificial priest as part of a fee. These forms of marriage were not well received in India or in the Caribbean during the indentureship period.

37. Bridget Brereton, *Race Relations in Colonial Trinidad, 1870–1900* (Cambridge: Cambridge University Press, 1979); Mohammed, "'Creolization' of Indian Women in Trinidad", 381–97; Hoefte, *In Place of Slavery*, 178.

38. See Rhoda Reddock, "Douglarization and the Politics of Gender Relations in Trinidad and Tobago: A Preliminary Exploration", in *Caribbean Sociology: Introductory Readings*, ed. Christine Barrow and Rhoda Reddock (Kingston: Ian Randle, 2001), 320–37.

39. Vatuk, "Protest Songs", 229.

40. Reddock, "Freedom Denied".

41. See Ravindra Jain, "Freedom Denied: Indian Women and Indentureship", *Economic and Political Weekly* 20 (1986): 79–87.

42. Emmer, "Great Escape", 248.

43. Moore, "Retention of Caste Notions", 101.

44. Raymond Williams and Edward Said, "Media, Margins and Modernity", in *The Politics of Modernism*, ed. Raymond Williams (London: Verso, 1989), 181.

45. Emmer, "The Great Escape", 254.

46. Reddock, "Freedom Denied."

47. G.C. Spivak, "Can the Subaltern Speak?", in *Marxism and Interpretation of Culture*, ed. Cary Nelson and Larry Grossberg (Hemel Hempstead: Harvester Wheatsheaf, 1988), 271–313.

48. Ibid.; Liddle and Joshi, *Daughters of Independence*, 25.

49. Bhabha, *Location of Culture*, 38–39.

50. Ibid., 112.

51. Kanhai, *Matikor*, 1–2.

52. Bhabha, *Location of Culture*.

53. Jenny Sharpe, "Figures of Colonial Resistance", *Modern Fiction Studies* 35, no. 1 (1989): 137.

Conclusion

1. Kay Saunders, *Workers in Bondage: The Origins and Bases of Unfree Labour in Queensland, 1824–1916* (London: University of Queensland Press, 1982), 151.

2. Luckhoo, "East Indians in British Guiana", 56.

3. Rodney, *How Europe Underdeveloped Africa*; Walter Rodney, "Upper Guinea and the Significance of the Origins of Africans Enslaved in the New World", *Journal of Negro History* 54 (1969): 327–45.

4. Eric Williams, *Capitalism and Slavery* (Chapel Hill: University of North Carolina Press, 1966).

5. In Niehoff and Niehoff, *East Indians*, 29.

6. James Rodway, "Labor and Colonization", *Timehri: Being the Journal of Royal Agricultural and Commercial Society of British Guiana* 6 (1911): 36.

7. Williams, *From Columbus to Castro*, 351.

8. Potter, "Post-Indenture Experience", 74.

9. Despres, *Cultural Pluralism*, 61.
10. E.C. Stembridge, "Indian Immigration to British Guiana", *United Empire*, new ser., 5, no. 1 (1914): 76.
11. George Lamming, "The West Indian People", *New World Quarterly* 2, no. 1 (1996): 69.
12. Harinder Singh Sohal, "The East Indian Indentureship System in Jamaica, 1845–1917" (PhD diss., University of Waterloo, 1978), 134.
13. Williams, *From Columbus to Castro*, 356.
14. Niehoff and Niehoff, *East Indians*, 38.
15. Edgar Mittelholzer, *Corentyne Thunder* (London: Eyre and Spottiswode, 1941).
16. E.A. Luckhoo, "East Indians in British Guiana", *Timehri: Being the Journal of Royal Agricultural and Commercial Society of British Guiana*, 3rd ser., 19 (1912): 312.
17. Arya, *Ritual Songs*, 157–58.
18. Laurence, *Question of Labor*, 515.
19. Potter, "Post-Indenture Experience", 74; Smith, "Some Characteristics".
20. Marina Carter, *Voices from Indenture: Experiences of Indian Migrants in the British Empire* (London: Leicester University Press, 1996), 80.
21. Haraksingh, "Control and Resistance".
22. A. Josa, "Hindus in the West Indies", *Timehri: Being the Journal of the Royal Agricultural and Commercial Society*, 3rd ser., 2, no. 19B (1912): 307.
23. Luckhoo, "East Indians in British Guiana", 61.
24. Comins, *Notes on Emigration from India to British Guiana*, 9.

Bibliography

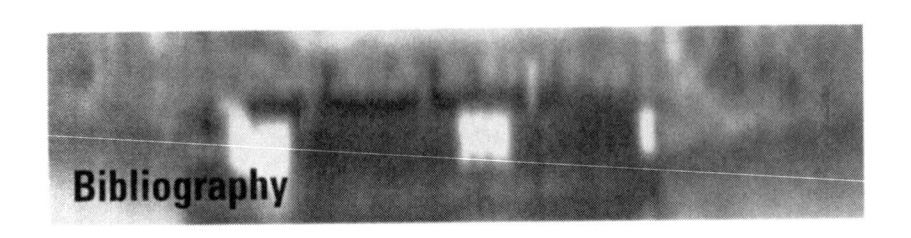

Primary Sources

Census of India. Vol. 1, part 1. 1921.

Comins, D.W.D. *Notes on Emigration from India to British Guiana.* Calcutta: Bengal Secretariat, 1893.

———. *Notes on Emigration from India to British Guiana, Trinidad, St Lucia and on Return Passage.* Calcutta: Bengal Secretariat, 1893.

———. *Notes on Emigration from India to Jamaica.* Calcutta: Bengal Secretariat, 1893.

———. *Notes on Emigration from India to Surinam.* Calcutta: Bengal Secretariat, 1893.

———. *Notes on Emigration from India to Trinidad.* Calcutta: Bengal Secretariat, 1893.

Denmark. Danish National Archives. Rigstarkivet. Vest Indiske Lokalarkiver. *The Coolie Journal* [English]. Ref. 3.81.584. Copenhagen, 1863.

India Record Office. *Bengal Emigration Proceedings.* British Library, London. Various years (October 1860–March 1866).

———. *Bengal Hurkaru.* British Library, London. Various dates (July–December 1838).

———. *India Emigration Proceedings.* Annual Reports of the Protector of Emigrants at Calcutta for December 1873–74. London, British Library.

———. *India Emigration Proceedings.* London, British Library. Various dates (August 1871–1878).

McNeill, James and Chimman Lal. *Report to the Government of India on the Conditions of Indian Immigrants in Four British Colonies and Suriname.* Part 1: Trinidad and British Guiana. London: HMSO, 1915.

United Kingdom. House of Commons. *Parliamentary Papers: The Twenty-third General Report of the Colonial Land and Emigration Commissioners*. Vol. 22 (3010). London: HMSO, 1862.

———. House of Commons. *Parliamentary Papers: The Twenty-fifth General Report of the Colonial Land and Emigration Commissioners*. Vol. 18 (3526). London: HMSO, 1865.

———. House of Commons. *Parliamentary Papers: The Twenty-sixth General Report of the Colonial Land and Emigration Commissioners*. Vol. 17 (3679). London: HMSO, 1866.

———. House of Commons. *Parliamentary Papers: The Twenty-ninth General Report of the Colonial Land and Emigration Commissioners*. London: HMSO, 1869.

———. House of Commons. *Parliamentary Papers: Report by Geoghegan on Immigration from India*. Vol. 47 (C. 314). London: HMSO, 1874.

———. House of Commons. *Parliamentary Papers: Report of the Committee from India to the Crown Colonies and Protectorates (Sanderson Committee)*. Vol. 27 (Cd. 5192–94). London: HMSO, 1910.

United Kingdom. India Office Records. *Bengal Emigration Proceedings*. London, 1860–1866.

———. India Office Records. *Bengal Hurkaru* [newspaper]. Calcutta, July–December 1838.

———. India Office Records. *Census of India, 1921*. Vol. 1, Part 1. London, 1921.

———. India Office Records. *India Emigration Proceedings*. London, 1871–1878.

United Kingdom. Public Records Office. Colonial Office. *British Guiana: Emigration*. No. 31. London, 1860.

———. Public Records Office. Colonial Office. *Government Emigration for Trinidad*. London, 1904.

———. Public Records Office. Colonial Office. Various Letters and Notes. 1860–1915.

Secondary Sources

Adamson, Alan H. *Sugar Without Slaves: The Political History of British Guiana, 1834–1904*. New Haven: Yale University Press, 1972.

Adas, Michael. *Prophets of Rebellion: Millenarian Protest against European Colonial Order*. Chapel Hill: University of North Carolina Press, 1979.

Altekar, A.S. *The Position of Women in Hindu Civilization*. Delhi: Motilal Banarsidass, 1962.

Ambiragan, S. "Malthusian Population Theory and Indian Famine Policy in the Nineteenth Century". *Population Studies* 30, no. 1 (1976): 5–14.

Andrews, C.F. "India's Emigration Problem". *Foreign Affairs* 8, no. 3 (1930): 430–49.

Arya, Usharbudh. *Ritual Songs and Folksongs of the Hindus Of Surinam.* Leiden: E.J. Brill, 1968.

Bacchus, M.K. *Education and Socio-Cultural Integration in a Plural Society.* Montreal: McGill University, Centre for Developing Area Studies, Occasional Paper Series, no. 6, 1970.

Bailey, Frederick G. "The Joint Family in India: A Framework for Discussion". *Economic Weekly* 12 (1960): 345–52.

Balzac, Honoré de. *A Harlot High and Low.* Translated by Reyner Happenstall. Harmondsworth: Penguin, 1970.

Barnes, Harry Elmer. *The History of Western Civilization.* Vol. 1. New York: Harcourt, Brace, 1935.

Basham, A.L. *Studies in Indian History and Culture.* Calcutta: Sambodhi, 1964.

———. *The Wonder That India Was.* 3rd ed. New York: Traplinger, 1968.

Bayly, Susan. *The New Cambridge History of India.* Vol. 3: *Caste, Society and Politics in India from the Eighteenth Century to the Modern Age.* Cambridge: Cambridge University Press, 1999.

Benedict, Burton. "Caste in Mauritius". In *Caste in Overseas Indian Communities*, edited by Barton M. Schwartz, 21–42. San Francisco: Chandler, 1967.

Bhabha, K. Homi. *The Location of Culture.* London: Routledge, 1994.

Bhasin, Kamala. *The Position of Women in India.* Bombay: Leslie Sawhany Programme of Training for Democracy, 1973.

Birbalsingh, Frank, ed. *Jahaji: An Anthology of Indo-Caribbean Fiction.* Toronto: Tsar, 2000.

———. *The Rise of West Indian Cricket: From Colony to Nation.* London: Hansib, 1996.

Bisnauth, Dale. *The Settlement of Indians in Guyana, 1890–1930.* Leeds: Peepal Tree Press, 2001.

Bolland, Nigel. "Systems of Dominations after Slavery: The Control of Land and Labor in British West Indies after 1838". *Comparative Studies in Society and History* 23, no. 4 (1981): 591–619.

Braithwaite, Lloyd. "Social Stratification and Cultural Pluralism". *Annals of the New York Academy of Sciences* 83 (1960): 816–31.

Brehm, Sharon S., and Jack W. Brehm. *Psychological Reactance. A Theory of Freedom and Control.* New York: Academic Press, 1981.

Brereton, Bridget. "The Experience of Indentureship: 1845–1917". In *Calcutta to Caroni: The East Indians in Trinidad*, edited by John G. La Guerre, 26–39. London: Longman, 1974.

———. *Race Relations in Colonial Trinidad, 1870–1900.* Cambridge: Cambridge University Press, 1979.

Bronkhurst, H.V.P. *Among the Hindus and Creoles of British Guiana.* London: T. Woolmer, 1888.

Burawoy, Micheal. "The Functions and Reproduction of Migrant Labor: Comparative Material from Southern Africa and the United States". *American Journal of Sociology* 8, no. 5 (1976): 1050–87.

Burke, Kenneth. *Attitudes toward History*. Los Altos, Calif.: Hermes, 1984.
Bush, Michael L. *Servitude in Modern Times*. Cambridge: Polity Press, 2000.
Carter, Marina. *Voices from Indenture: Experiences of Indian Migrants in the British Empire*. London: Leicester University Press, 1996.
Carter, Mirina, and Khal Torabully. *Coolitude: An Anthology of Indian Labor Diaspora*. London: Anthem Press, 2002.
Chanderbali, David. "A Guyanese Perspective". Proceedings of the international seminar From Indentureship to Entrepreneurship: East Indians and the Socio-Economic Transition in the Caribbean, University of the West Indies, St Augustine. Trinidad, 2003.
Channa, Dev Raj. *Slavery in Ancient India*. New Delhi: People's Publishing House, 1960.
Cheng, Lucie, and Edna Bonacich, eds. *Labor Immigration Under Capitalism*. Los Angeles: University of California Press, 1984.
Childs, Peter, and Patrick Williams. *An Introduction to Post-Colonial Theory*. London: Prentice Hall, 1997.
Clarke, Colin. "Caste among Hindus in a Town in San Fernando". In *Caste in Overseas Indian Communities*, edited by Barton M. Schwartz, 165–99. San Francisco: Chandler, 1967.
Clementi-Ojha, C. "Outside the Norms: Women Ascetics in Hindu Society". *Economic and Political Weekly* 23, no. 18 (1988): 34–36.
Crowley, Daniel. "Cultural Assimilation in a Multiracial Society". *Annals of the New York Academy of Sciences* 83 (1960): 850–54.
———. "Plural and Differential Acculturation in Trinidad". *American Anthropologist* 57 (1957): 817–24.
Cumpston, I.M. "Survey of Indian Immigration to British Tropical Colonies to 1910". *Population Studies* 10, no. 2 (1956): 158–65.
Dabydeen, David. *Coolie Odyssey*. London: Hansib, 1988.
Dabydeen, David, and Brinsley Samaroo. Introduction to *Across Dark Waters: Ethnicity and Indian Identity in the Caribbean*, edited by David Dabydeen and Brinsley Samaroo, 1–11. London: Macmillan, 1996.
———, eds. *India in the Caribbean*. London: Hansib, 1987.
Datta, K. *Survey of India's Social Life and Economic Conditions in the Eighteenth Century (1707–1813)*. Calcutta: Firma, 1961.
Davids, Leo. "The East Indian Family Overseas". *Social and Economic Studies* 13 (1964): 383–96.
Deka, Usha. "Early Instances of Race-Crossing in India". *Man in India* 43, no. 4 (1954): 271–76.
Desai, I.P. "The Joint Family in India: An Analysis". *Sociological Bulletin* 5 (1956): 144–56.
Despres, Leo A. "Anthropology, Cultural Pluralism and the Study of Complex Societies". *Cultural Anthropology* 9, no. 1 (1968): 3–26.
———. *Cultural Pluralism and Nationalist Politics in British Guiana*. Chicago: Rand McNally, 1967.

Douglas, Federick. *My Bondage and My Freedom.* Edited and with an introduction by William L. Andrews. Urbana: University of Illinois Press, 1987.

Duiker, William J., and Jackson J. Spielvogel. *World History.* 4th ed. Belmont, Calif.: Thomson and Wadsworth, 2003.

Durkhiem, Emile. *The Division of Labour in Society.* New York: Free Press, 1964.

Dutt, Romesh. *The Economic History of India.* New York: A.M. Kelly, 1969.

Eliot, George. *Adam Bede.* 1859. Reprint, Harmondsworth: Penguin, 1981.

Emmer, Pieter. "The Great Escape: The Migration of Female Indentured Servants from British India to Surinam, 1873–1916". In *Abolition and Its Aftermath,* edited by P.D. Richardson, 245–66. London: Frank Cass, 1986.

Erickerson. Eric L. "Introduction of East Indian Coolies into the British West Indies". *Journal of Modern History* 6 (1934): 127–46.

Evansohn, E. "Workers and Imperialism: Where is the Aristocracy of Labor". *Insurgent Sociologist* 7, no. 2 (1977): 54–63.

Fanon, Frantz. *The Wretched of the Earth.* New York: Grove Press, 1968.

Forbes, Geraldine. *Women in India.* Cambridge: Cambridge University Press, 1996.

Foucault, Michel. *The Archaeology of Knowledge.* Translated by A.M. Sheridan Smith. New York: Pantheon Books, 1972.

———. *The History of Sexuality: An Introduction.* Vol. 1. Translated by R. Hurley. New York: Vintage Books, 1980.

Frazier, Franklin. *The Negro Family in the United States.* Chicago: University of Chicago Press, 1939.

Freud, Sigmund. "Humor". *Inter-journal of Psycho-Analysis* 9 (1928): 1–6.

Furnivall, J.S. *Colonial Policy and Practice: A Comparative Study of Burma and Netherlands India.* Cambridge: Cambridge University Press, 1948.

Galenson, David W. *White Servitude in Colonial America.* Cambridge: Cambridge University Press, 1981.

Gallagher, J., and Ronald Robinson. "The Imperialism of Free Trade". *Economic History Review* 6, no. 1 (1953): 1–15.

Gillion, K.L. *Fiji's Indian Emigrant.* London: Oxford University Press, 1962.

———. "The Sources of Indian Emigration to Fiji". *Population Studies* 10 (1956): 139–57.

Gobineau, Arthur (Count Joseph Arthur de Gobineau), and Adrian Collins. *The Inequality of Human Races.* 2nd ed. Reprint, Torrance, Calif.: Noontide Press, 1983.

Gosine, Mahin, and Dhanpaul Narine. *Sojourners to Settlers: The Indian Immigrants in the Caribbean and the Americas.* New York: Windsor Press, 1999.

Goveia, Elsa. *Slave Society in the British Leeward Islands at the End of the Eighteenth Century.* New Haven: Yale University Press, 1965.

Gramsci, Antonio. *Selections from the Prison Notebooks.* Edited and translated by Quinten Hoare and Geoffry Nowell Smith. London: Wishart, 1971.

Green, William. *British Slave Emancipation: The Sugar Colonies and the Great Experiment, 1830–1865.* Oxford: Clarendon, 1976.
Grierson, George A. *Report on Colonial Emigration from Bengal Presidency.* Calcutta: Bengal Secretariat, 1883.
Haraksingh, Kusha. "Control and Resistance among Indian Workers: A Study of Labour on the Sugar Plantations of Trinidad, 1875–1917". In *India in the Caribbean*, edited by David Dabydeen and Brinsley Samaroo, 61–80. London: Hansib, 1987.
Heath, Roy. *The Shadow Bride.* New York: Persa Books, 1996.
Henriques, Fernando. *Family and Colour in Jamaica.* London: MacGibbon and Kee, 1953.
Henslin, James, ed. *Essentials of Sociology: A Down to Earth Approach.* 4th ed. Boston: Allyn and Bacon, 2003.
Herskovits, Melville. *The Myth of the Negro Past.* New York: Harpers, 1941.
Hiejle, B. "Slavery and Agriculture Bondage in South India in the Nineteenth Century". *Scandinavian Economic History Review* 15, no. 1–2 (1967): 71–126.
Higman, B.W. *Slave Population and Economy in Jamaica, 1807–1834.* Cambridge: Cambridge University Press, 1976.
Hobsbawn, Eric. "Peasants and Politics". *Journal of Peasant Studies* 1, no. 1 (1973): 3–22.
Hoefte, Rosemarijin. *In Place of Slavery: A Social History of British Indian and Javanese Laborers in Suriname.* Gainesville: University Press of Florida, 1998.
Hoggart, Richard. *The Use of Literacy: Aspects of the Working Class Life.* London: Chatto and Windus, 1954.
hooks, bell. *Yearning: Race, Gender, and Cultural Politics.* Boston: South End Press, 1990.
Hutton, J.H. *Caste in India.* London: Oxford University Press, 1951.
Inden, Roland. *Imagining India.* Oxford: Basil Blackwell, 1990.
Jain, Ravindra. "Freedom Denied: Indian Women and Indentureship". *Economic and Political Weekly* 20 (1986): 79–87.
Jayawardena, Chandra. *Conflict and Solidarity in a Guianese Plantation.* London: University of London, Athlone, 1963.
———. "Ideology and Conflict in Lower Class Communities". *Comparative Studies in Society and History* 10 (1968): 413–46.
Jenkins, Ron. *Subversive Laughter: The Liberating Power of Comedy.* Toronto: The Free Press, 1994.
Jenson, Peter H. *From Serfdom to Fireburn and Strike: A History of Black Labour in the Danish West Indies, 1848–1916.* St Croix, US Virgin Islands: Antilles Press, 1998.
Jha, J.C. "The Indian Heritage in Trinidad". In *Calcutta to Caroni: The East Indians in Trinidad*, edited by John G. La Guerre, 1–24. London: Longman, 1974.
———. "The Indian Mutiny-cum-Revolt of 1857 and Trinidad (West Indies)". *Indian Studies: Past and Present* 13, no. 4 (1972): 419–30.
Josa, A. "Hindus in the West Indies". *Timehri: Being the Journal of the Royal Agricultural and Commercial Society,* 3rd ser., 2, no. 19B (1912): 306–8.

Kale, Madhavi. *Fragments of Empire: Capital, Slavery and Indian Indentured Labor Migration in the British West Indies*. Philadelphia: University of Pennsylvania Press, 1998.

———. "Projecting Identities: Empire and Indentured Labor Migration from India to Trinidad and British Guiana, 1836–1885". In *Nation and Migration*, edited by Peter van der Veer, 73–92. Philadelphia: University of Pennsylvania Press, 1995.

Kanhai, Rosanne, ed. *Matikor: The Politics of Identity for Indo-Caribbean Women*. St Augustine, Trinidad: University of the West Indies, School of Continuing Studies, 1999.

Khare, R.S. *The Untouchable as Himself: Ideology, Identity, and Pragmatism among the Lucknow Chamars*. Cambridge Studies in Cultural Systems, no. 8, Cambridge: Cambridge University Press, 1984.

Kierkegaard, Soren. *Concluding Unscientific Postscript*, translated by David Swenson and Walter Lowrie. Princeton: Princeton University Press, 1941.

Klass, Morton. *East Indians in Trinidad: A Study of Cultural Persistence*. New York: Columbia University Press, 1961.

Knight, Franklin. *The Caribbean: The Genesis of a Fragmented Nationalism*. New York: Oxford University Press, 1990.

Kolenda, Pauline Mahar. "Region, Caste and Family Structure: A Comparative Study of the Indian 'Joint' Family". In *Structure and Change in Indian Society*, edited by Milton Singer and Benard S. Cohn, 339–96. Chicago: Adline, 1968.

Kondapi, C. *Indians Overseas, 1838–1949*. New Delhi: India Council of World Affairs, 1951.

Korom, Frank. *Hosay Trinidad*. Philadelphia: University of Pennsylvania Press, 2002.

Lal, Brij V. "Fiji Girmitiyas: The Background to Banishment". In *Rama's Banishment*, edited by Vijay Mishra, 12–39. Auckland: Heineman, 1979.

———. *Girmitiyas: The Origins of the Fiji Indians*. Canberra: Journal of Pacific History, 1983.

Lamming, George. "The West Indian People". *New World Quarterly* 2, no. 1 (1996): 63–74.

Lardiniois, Roland. "Famine, Epidemics and Mortality in South India: A Reappraisal of the Demographic Crisis of 1876–1878". *Economic and Political Weekly* 20, no. 11 (1985): 454–65.

Laurence, Keith. *A Question of Labor: Indentured Immigration into Trinidad and British Guiana, 1875–1917*. New York: St Martin's Press, 1994.

Lenin, V.I. *The Highest Stage of Capitalism*. New York: Praeger, 1973.

Lenksi, Gerhard, and Jean Lenski. *Human Societies: An Introduction to Macrosociology*, 5th ed. New York: McGraw-Hill, 1987.

Levine, Laurence. *Black Culture and Black Consciousness: Afro-American Folk Thought from Slavery to Freedom*. Oxford: Oxford University Press, 1977.

Liddle, Joanna, and Rama Joshi. *Daughters of Independence: Gender, Caste, and Class in India*. New Brunswick, NJ: Rutgers University Press, 1986.

———. "Gender and Imperialism in British India". *Economic and Political Weekly* 20, no. 43 (1985): 72–78.

Look Lai, Walton. *Indentured Labor, Caribbean Sugar: Chinese and Indian Migrants to the British West Indies, 1838–1917.* Baltimore: Johns Hopkins University Press, 1993.

Lowenthal, David. *West Indian Societies.* New York: Oxford University Press, 1972.

Lublin, Joann. "Women at Top are Distant from CEO Jobs". *Wall Street Journal.* 28 February 1996, B1.

Luckhoo, E.A. "East Indians in British Guiana". *Timehri: Being the Journal of Royal Agricultural and Commercial Society of British Guiana*, 3rd ser., 2, no. 19B (1912): 309–14.

———. "The East Indians in British Guiana: From Their Advent to this Colony to the Present Time: A Survey of the Economic, Educational and Political Aspects". *Timehri: Being the Journal of Royal Agricultural and Commercial Society of British Guiana*, 3rd ser., 6, no. 23 (1919): 53–65.

Macionis, J. John. *Sociology.* 10th edition. Upper Saddle River, NJ: Prentice Hall, 2005.

Mahabir, Noorkumar. *The Still Cry: Personal Accounts of East Indians in Trinidad and Tobago During Indentureship (1845–1917).* Ithaca, NY: Calaloux, 1985.

Malik, Yogendra K. *East Indians in Trinidad.* London: Oxford University Press, 1971.

Mandel, Ernest. "The Laws of Uneven Development". *New Left Review* 59 (1970): 19–40.

Mandelbaum, David. *Society in India.* Berkeley and Los Angeles: University of California Press, 1970.

Mangru, Basdeo. *Benevolent Neutrality: Indian Government Policy and Labor Migration to British Guiana, 1854–1884.* London: Hansib, 1987.

———. *A History of East Indian Resistance on the Guyana Sugar Estates, 1869–1948.* New York: Mellon, 1996.

Mansingh, Lakshmi, and Ajai Mansingh. *Home Away from Home: 150 Years of Indian Presence in Jamaica, 1845–1995.* Kingston: Ian Randle, 2000.

Manuel, Peter. *East Indian Music in the West Indies: Tan-Singing, Chutney and the Making of Indo-Caribbean Culture.* Philadelphia: Temple University Press, 2000.

Marx, Karl, and Friedrich Engels. *The Communist Manifesto.* 1848. Reprint, England: Harmondsworth, 1967.

Mazumdar, S. "Colonial Impact and Punjabi Emigration to the United States". In *Labor Immigration Under Capitalism: Asian Workers in the United States before World War II,* edited by Lucie Cheng and Edna Bonacich, 316–36. Los Angeles: University of California Press, 1984.

Metcalf, Thomas R. *The Aftermath of Revolt, India 1857–1877.* Princeton, NJ: Princeton University Press, 1964.

Metha, Brinda. *Diasporic (Dis)locations: Indo-Caribbean Women Writers Negotiate the Kala Pani.* Kingston: University of the West Indies Press, 2004.

Michaelson, Maureen. "Caste, Kinship and Marriage: A Study of Two Gujarati Trading Castes in England". PhD thesis, University of London (SOAS), 1983.
Mintz, Sidney. "The Origins of Reconstituted Peasantries". In *Caribbean Transformation*, edited by Sidney Mintz, 146–56. Baltimore: Johns Hopkins University Press, 1974.
Mittelholzer, Edgar. *Corentyne Thunder.* London: Eyre and Spottiswode, 1941.
Mohammed, Patricia. "The 'Creolization' of Indian Women in Trinidad". In *The Independence Experience, 1962–1987*, edited by Selwyn Ryan, 381–97. St Augustine, Trinidad: University of the West Indies, 1988.
Mohapatra, Prabhu, P. "Restoring the Family: Wife Murders and the Making of a Sexual Contract for Indian Immigrant Labor in the British Caribbean Colonies, 1860–1920". *Studies in History* 11, no. 2 (1995): 228–60.
Moore, Barrington, Jr. *Injustice: The Social Bases of Obedience and Revolt.* White Plains, New York: M.E. Sharpe, 1987.
Moore, Brian. *Race, Power and Social Segmentation in Colonial Society: Guyana After Slavery, 1838–1891.* New York: Gordon and Breach, 1987.
———. "The Retention of Caste Notions among the Indian Immigrants in British Guiana During the Nineteenth Century". *Comparative Studies in Society and History* 19 (1977): 96–107.
Morgan, Lewis Henry. *Ancient Society.* 1877. Foreword by Elizabeth Tooker. Reprint, Tucson: University of Arizona Press, 1985.
Morreall, John, ed. *The Philosophy of Laughter and Humor.* Albany: State University of New York Press, 1987.
Morris, H.S. "Caste among Indians of Uganda". In *Caste in Overseas Indian Communities*, edited by Barton M. Schwartz, 267–82. San Francisco: Chandler, 1967.
Morton, Sarah. *John Morton of Trinidad.* Toronto: Westminster, 1916.
Mukhopadhyay, Maitrayee. *Silver Shackles: Women and Development in India.* Oxford: Oxfam, 1984.
Naipaul, V.S. *Between Father and Son: Family Letters.* New York: Knopf, 2000.
Najita, Tetsuo, and Irwin Scheiner. *Japanese Thought in the Tokugawa Period, 1600–1868: Methods and Metaphors.* Chicago: University of Chicago Press, 1978.
Nath, Dwarka. *History of Indians in British Guiana.* London, New York: Nelson, 1975.
Naylor, Larry. *Culture and Change: An Introduction.* Westport, Conn.: Bergin and Garvey, 1996.
Nehru, Jawaharlal. *The Discovery of India* Oxford: Oxford University Press, 1989.
Nevadomsky, Joseph. "Changes in Hindu Institutions in an Alien Environment". *Eastern Anthropologist* 33, no. 1 (1980): 39–53.
———. "Changes Over Time and Space in the East Indian Family in Rural Trinidad". *Journal of Comparative Family Studies* 11, no. 4 (1980): 434–36.
Nicholas, Ralph W. "Structures of Politics in the Indian Villages of Southern Asia". In *Structure and Change in Indian Society*, edited by Milton Singer and Bernard S. Cohen, 243–63. Chicago: Aldine, 1968.

Niehoff, Arthur, and Jaunita Niehoff. *East Indians in the West Indies*. Milwaukee: Milwaukee Public Museum, Publication in Anthropology no. 6, 1960.
Northrup, David. *Indentured Labour in the Age of Imperialism, 1834–1922*. Cambridge: Cambridge University Press, 1995.
Omvedt, Gail. "Migration in Colonial India: The Articulation of Feudalism and Capitalism by the Colonial State". *Journal of Peasant Studies* 7 (1980): 185–212.
———. "Towards a Theory of Colonialism". *Insurgent Sociologist* 3 (1973): 1–24.
Parry, P.H., and Phillip Sherlock. *The Short History of the West Indies*. London: Macmillan, 1982.
Patterson, Orlando. *Slavery and Social Death: A Comparative Study*. Cambridge: Harvard University Press, 1982.
———. *The Sociology of Slavery*. London: MacGibbon and Kee, 1967.
Petras, E.M. "Towards a Theory of International Labor: The New Division of Labor". In *Sourcebook on the New Immigration*, edited by Roy Bryce-Laporte, 434–49. Washington: DC, Smithsonian Institution, Research Institute on Immigration and Ethnic Studies, 1979.
Phillips, L.H.C. "Single Men in Barracks: Some Memories of Plantation Life". *Timehri: Being the Journal of Royal Agricultural and Commercial Society of British Guiana*, 4th ser., 40 (1961): 23–34.
Portes, A. "Migration and Underdevelopment". *Politics and Society* 8, no. 1 (1978): 1–48.
Potter, Lesily M. "The Post-Indenture Experience of East Indians in Guyana, 1871–1922". In *Indenture and Exile: The Indo-Caribbean Experience*, edited by Frank Birbalsingh, 71–92. Toronto: Tsar, 1989.
Poynting, Jeremy. "East Indian Women in the Caribbean: Experience and Voice". In *India in the Caribbean*, edited by David Dabydeen and Brinsley Samaroo, 231–61. London: Hansib, 1987.
Premdas, Ralph. "Diversity and Liberation in the Caribbean: The Decentralist Policy Challenge in the New Millennium". In *Contending with Destiny: The Caribbean in the Twenty-first Century*, edited by Kenneth Hall and Denis Benn, 161–78. Kingston: Ian Randle, 2000.
Ragatz, L.J. *The Fall of the Planter Class in the British Caribbean, 1763–1833*. New York: Octagon, 1971.
Ramdin, Ron. *Arising from Bondage: A History of Indo-Caribbean People*. New York: New York University Press, 2000.
Ramesar, Marianne. *Survivors of Another Crossing: A History of East Indians in Trinidad, 1880–1946*. St Augustine, Trinidad: University of West Indies Press, 1994.
Ramnarine, Tina K. *Creating Their Own Space: The Development of an Indian-Caribbean Musical Tradition*. Kingston: University of the West Indies Press, 2001.
Ramnarine, Tyran. "Over a Hundred Years of East Indian Disturbances on the Sugar Estates of Guyana, 1869–1978: An Historical Overview". In *India in the Caribbean*, edited by David Dabydeen and Brinsley Samaroo, 119–44. London: Hansib, 1987.

Reckless, Walter C. *The Crime Problem*. 5th ed. New York: Appleton, 1973.

Reddock, Rhoda. "Douglarization and the Politics of Gender Relations in Trinidad and Tobago: A Preliminary Exploration". In *Caribbean Sociology: Introductory Readings*, edited by Christine Barrow and Rhoda Reddock, 320–37. Kingston: Ian Randle, 2001.

———. "Freedom Denied! Indian Women and Indentureship in Trinidad and Tobago, 1854–1917". *Economic and Political Weekly* 20, no. 43 (1985): 79–87.

Renard, Rosamunde A. "Labour Relations in Post-Slavery Martinique and Guadeloupe, 1858–1870". In *Caribbean Freedom: Economy and Society from Emancipation to the Present*, edited by Hilary Beckles and Verene Shepherd, 161–67. Kingston: Ian Randle, 1996.

Repak, Terry A. "Labor Recruitment and the Lure of the Capital: Central American Migrants in Washington, DC". *Gender and Society* 8, no. 4 (1994): 507–21.

———. *Working on Washington: Central American Workers in the Nation's Capital*. Philadelphia: Temple University Press, 1995.

Risely, H.H. *The Tribes and Castes of Bengal*. Vol. 2. Calcutta: Bengal Secretariat Press, 1892.

Robert, G.W., and J. Byrne. "Summary Statistics on Indenture and Associated Migration Affecting the West Indies, 1834–1918". *Population Studies* 20 (1966): 125–34.

Rodney, Walter. *A History of Guyanese Working People, 1881–1904*. Baltimore: Johns Hopkins University Press, 1981.

———. *How Europe Underdeveloped Africa*. Washington, DC: Howard University Press, 1981.

———. "Upper Guinea and the Significance of the Origins of Africans Enslaved in the New World", *Journal of Negro History* 54 (1969): 327–45.

Rodway, James. "Labor and Colonization". *Timehri: Being the Journal of Royal Agricultural and Commercial Society of British Guiana* 6 (1911): 21–42.

Roopnarine, Lomarsh. "Creating Opportunities out of Indo-Caribbean Indenture". Paper presented at the conference on Globalization, Diaspora and Identity Formation, Paramaribo, Suriname. February 2004.

———. "Indo-Caribbean Intra-Island Migration: Not so marginalized!" *Social and Economic Studies* 54, no. 2 (2005): 107–36.

———. "Indo-Caribbean Migration from Periphery to Core". *Caribbean Quarterly* 49, no. 3 (2003): 30–60.

———. "Indo-Caribbean Social Identity", *Caribbean Quarterly* 52, no. 1 (2006): 1–11.

———. "Indo-Guyanese Migration: From Plantation to Metropolis". *Immigrants and Minorities* 20, no. 2 (2001): 1–25.

———. "Return Migration of Indentured East Indians from the Caribbean to India, 1838–1920". *Journal of Caribbean History* 40, no. 2 (2006): 308–24.

Rosengarten, Theodore. *All God's Danger: The Life of Nate Shaw*. New York: Knopf, 1974.

Rothermund, Dietmar. "Government, Landlord and Tenant in India, 1875–1900". *Indian Economic and Social History Review* 6 (1969): 351–67.
Said, Edward. *Orientalism*. Harmondsworth: Penguin, 1978.
———. *The World, the Text and the Critic*. London: Faber and Faber, 1984.
Saha, P. *Emigration of Indian Labor, 1834–1900*. New Delhi: People's Publishing House, 1970.
Samaroo, Brinsley. "In Sick Longing for the Further Shore: Return Migration by Caribbean East Indians During the Nineteenth and Twentieth Centuries". In *Return Migration and Remittances: Developing A Caribbean Perspective*, edited by William F. Stiner, Klaus de Albquerque, and Roy S. Bryce-Laporte, 45–72. Riies Occasional Papers, no. 3, Research Institute on Immigration and Ethnic Studies Smithsonian Institution, Washington, DC, 1982.
Sandhu, K.S. *Indians in Malaya: Some Aspects of their Immigration and Settlement 1786–1957*. Cambridge: Cambridge University Press, 1969.
Saunders, Kay. *Workers in Bondage: The Origins and Bases of Unfree Labour in Queensland, 1824–1916*. London: University of Queensland Press, 1982.
Scott, C. James. *Domination and the Arts of Resistance: Hidden Transcript*. New Haven: Yale University Press, 1990.
———. *Weapons of the Weak: Everyday Forms of Peasant Resistance*. New Haven: Yale University Press, 1985.
Seecharan, Clem. *Bechu: "Bound Coolie" Radical in British Guiana, 1894–1901*. Kingston: University of the West Indies Press, 1999.
———. *India and the Shaping of Indo-Guyanese Imagination, 1890s–1920s*. Leeds: Peepal Tree Press, 1993.
———. "The Shaping of the Indo-Caribbean People in the 1940s". *Journal of Caribbean Studies* 14, no. 2 (2000): 61–92.
———. *Sweetening "Bitter Sugar": Jock Campbell, The Booker Reformer in British Guiana, 1934–66*. Kingston: Ian Randle, 2004.
———. *Tiger in the Stars: The Anatomy of Indian Achievement in British Guiana, 1919–1929*. Warwick University Caribbean Studies. London: Macmillian, 1997.
Seenarine, M. *Indentured Indian Women in Colonial Guyana: Recruitment, Migration, Labor and Caste*. http://saxakali.com/indocarib/sojourner3.htm, 1999.
Senart, Emile. *Caste in India: Facts and the System*. Translated by Sir E. Denison Ross. London: Methuen, 1930.
Shahani, Savitri. "The Joint Family: A Case Study". *Economic Weekly* 13 (1961): 1823–28.
Sharpe, Jenny. "Figures of Colonial Resistance". *Modern Fiction Studies* 35, no. 1 (1989): 137–55.
Shepherd, Verene. *Maharani's Misery: Narratives of a Passage from India*. Kingston: University of the West Indies Press, 2002.
———. *Transients to Settlers: The Experience of Indians in Jamaica 1845–1950*. Leeds: Peepal Tree Press, 1994.
———. *Women in Caribbean History*. Kingston: Ian Randle, 1999.

Shineberg, Dorothy. *The People Trade: Pacific Island Laborers and New Caledonia, 1865–1930*. Honolulu: University of Hawaii Press, 1999.

Singer, Milton. "The Indian Joint Family in Modern Industry". In *Structure and Change in Indian Society*, edited by Milton Singer and Benard S. Cohn, 432–52. Chicago: Adline, 1968.

Singh, Kelvin. *Bloodstained Tombs: The Muharram Massacre, 1884*. London and Basingstoke: Macmillan, 1988.

———. "East Indians and the Larger Society". In *Calcutta to Caroni: The East Indians in Trinidad*, edited by John G. La. Guerre, 39–68. London: Longman, 1974.

———. *Race and Class Struggles in a Colonial State: Trinidad, 1917–1945*. Calgary: University of Calgary and The Press, University of the West Indies, 1994.

Smith, Donald E. *India as a Secular State*. Princeton: Princeton University Press, 1963.

Smith, M.G. *The Plural Society in the West Indies*. Berkeley: University of California Press, 1965.

Smith, Raymond. *British Guiana*. London: Oxford University Press, 1962.

———. "Marriage and Family amongst East Indians in British Guiana". *Social and Economic Studies* 8, no. 4 (1959): 321–76.

———. "Social Stratification, Cultural Pluralism, and Integration in West Indian Societies". In *Caribbean Integration: Papers on Social, Political and Economic Integration*, edited by S. Lewis and T. G. Mathews, 226–58. Puerto Rico: University of Puerto Rice Press, 1967.

———. "Some Characteristics of Indian Immigrants to British Guiana". *Population Studies* 13, no. 1 (1959): 34–39.

Sohal, Harinder Singh. "The East Indian Indentureship System in Jamaica, 1845–1917". PhD Dissertation, Waterloo: Ontario, 1978.

Speckmann, Johan. *Marriage and Kinship among Indians in Suriname*. Assen: Van Gorcum, 1965.

Spivak, G.C. "Can the Subaltern Speak?" In *Marxism and Interpretation of Culture*, edited by Cary Nelson and Larry Grossberg, 271–313. Hemel Hempstead: Harvester Wheatsheaf, 1988.

Srivastava, H.S. *The History of Indian Famines and Development of Famine Policy, 1858–1918*. Delhi: Agra, 1967.

Stembridge. E.C. "Indian Immigration to British Guiana". *United Empire*, new ser., 5, no. 1 (1914): 72–78.

Sykes, Gresham M., and David Matza. "Techniques of Neutralization". In *Down to Earth Sociology: Introductory Readings*. 5th ed. Edited by James Henslin, 225–31. New York: Free Press, 1988.

Thorner, Daniel, and Alice Thorner. *Land and Labor in India*. Bombay: Asia Publishing House, 1962.

Tinker, Hugh. *A New System of Slavery: The Export of Indian Labour Overseas, 1830–1920*. Oxford: Institute of Race Relations, London, 1974.

Van der Veer, Peter, and Steve Vertevoc. "Brahmanism Abroad: On Caribbean Hinduism as an Ethnic Religion". *Ethnology* 30 (1991): 149–66.

Vatuk, Prakash V. "Protest Songs of East Indians in British Guiana". *Journal of American Folklore* 77, no. 305 (1964): 220–35.

Vertovec, Steve. *The Hindu Diaspora: Comparative Patterns*. London: Routledge, 2000.

———. *Hindu Trinidad: Religion, Ethnicity and Socio-Economic Change*. London: Macmillan, 1992.

Wagely, Charles. "Plantation America: A Culture Sphere". In *Caribbean Studies: A Symposium*, edited by Vera Rubin. 1–13. Seattle: University of Washington Press, 1960.

Walcott, Dereck. "The Antilles: Fragments of Epic Memory". Nobel Lecture. http://nobelprize.org/literature/laureates/1992/walcott-lecture.html

Wallerstein, Immanuel. *The Modern World-System, Capitalist Agriculture and the Origins of the European World-Economy in the Sixteenth Century*. New York: Academic Press, 1974.

Weller, Judith. *The East Indian Indenture in Trinidad*. Rio Piedras, Puerto Rico: Institute of Caribbean Studies, 1968.

Williams, Eric. *Capitalism and Slavery*. Chapel Hill: University of North Carolina Press, 1966.

———. *From Columbus to Castro: A History of the Caribbean, 1492–1969*. New York: Vintage Books, 1984.

Williams, Raymond, and Edward Said. "Media, Margins and Modernity". In *The Politics of Modernism*, edited by Raymond Williams, 177–298. London: Verso, 1989.

Wolf, Eric. *Peasant Wars in the Twentieth Century*. New York: Harper and Row, 1969.

Wolf, Eric, and Sidney Mintz. "Haciendas and Plantations in Middle America and the Antilles". *Social and Economic Studies* 6, no. 3 (1957): 380–412.

Wood, Charles H. "Equilibrium and Historical-Structural Perspective on Migration". *International Migration Review* 16, no. 2 (1982): 298–319.

Wood, Donald. *Trinidad in Trinidad*. London: Oxford University Press, 1968.

Yawney, Carole. "Drinking Patterns and Alcoholism in Trinidad". In *McGill Studies in Caribbean Anthropology*, edited by F. Henry, 34–48. Montreal: McGill University, 1969.

Index

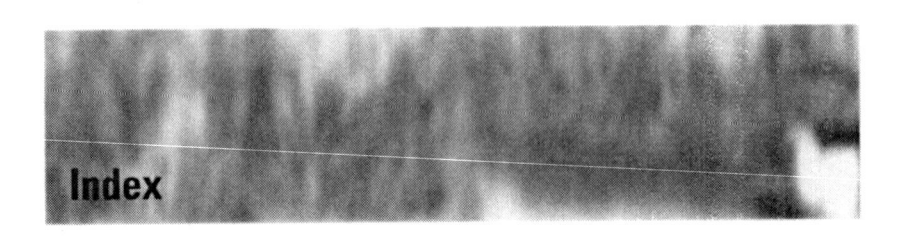

acculturation, and cultural continuity, 63
Action Theory, 63–64
Adamson, Alan, 51
alcoholism, 109
ankylostomiasis, 50
Aryans, 65
Arya Samaj (Association of the Respected Ones), 71, 90

Bechu, 4, 56, 70
Benedict, Burton, 65
Bhabha, Homi, 105
Black Culture and Black Consciousness (Levine), 53
Bloodstained Tombs: The Muharram Massacre, 1884 (Singh), 55–56
Braithwaite, Lloyd, 63–64
Brereton, B., 67
British colonial policy
    effect on Indian labour migration, 10, 13, 16–18, 109, 140n15
    in Egypt, 38–39
    on gender relations, 89–90, 104
    Sepoy Mutiny, 22–23
    socioeconomic oppression of, 17–20, 23, 26
British Guiana
    British Guiana East Indian Asociation, 73
    People's Association of British Guiana, 73
    rice industry in, 110
    sugar production in, 110
Bronkhurst, H.V.P., 68
Burbank, C., 22

Camp des Noirs, 72
capital accumulation, 15–17, 21
capitalism. *See* world capitalism
Caribbean colonial societies
    power and domination of planter class, 41–42
    rise in exports, 110
caste system
    Arya Samaj (Association of the Respected Ones), 71
    breakdown of in indentured communities, 72–76
    breakdown of in plantation system, 67–72
    caste composition of emigrants, 29

characteristics of, 65, 105
cultural changes to under indenture, 65–67, 69, 113–14, 116–17
as factor in emigration, 10, 11
as hindrance to emigration, 25–26
jati identity, 26, 69
and labour migration, 13, 22
loss of caste, 25, 68, 102
oppression under, 19
regaining caste status, 67–68
reversal of status in, 70–71
Sanatan Dharma (Eternal Religion), 71
transition to class system, 72–76
untouchables, 48, 65
"up-caste" of identity, 67
Chandra, Ishwar, 90
civil wars, as cause of emigration, 22–23
class system
emergence of, 76
transition of caste system to, 72–76
Cockerbell, H.A., 23
cocoa industry, 15
coffee industry, 15
colonialism
defined, 13
as economic vassalage, 17–20
emergence of, 38–39
evangelical colonialism, 70–71
intellectual dominance and, 39
and labour migration, 10, 13, 16–18, 109, 140n15
metropolitan-colonial relationship and, 15–17
as Social Darwinism, 14
Comins, D.W.D., 50, 68
The Communist Manifesto (Marx and Engels), 45
Control and Resistance Among Indian Workers (Haraksingh), 40
control theory on prevention of crime, 99
Corentyne Thunder (Mittelholzer), 111
creolization, 64
crime, control theory on prevention of, 99

crimping, 23–24, 32
cultural adaptivity, as form of resistance, 114–16
cultural change
African school compared to East Indian experience, 64
theories of, 62–65
cultural continuity, 10, 11
and acculturation, 63
and assimilation, 68
and intergenerational socioeconomic mobility, 62
religion and, 116, 146n61
cultural factors, as hindrance to emigration, 25–26
cultural supremacy, 36–37
culture hybridity, 105–6
culturist theory, on wife murder, 97–99

Deka, Usha, 27
Denmark, request for indentured labour, 7
desertion
as form of resistance, 50–51
and runaway communities, 51
Des Voeux (magistrate of British Guiana), 108
Devonshire Caste Disturbance (1872, British Guiana), 70
divorce, 65
dominance and domination
compliance and, 47
fear of mass revolt, 46
mimic individuals and, 107
origins of, 36–41
primary resistance, 49–53
resistance against, 36, 115–16
symbolic resistance, 49, 53–61
transcripts of power relations, 44–49
doogla, 102
Durkheim, Emile, 53, 64

East Indian National Association, 73
East Indian National Congress, 73
East Indians

adaptive capacity of, 109–10, 119–20
age of emigrants, 27
Caribbean recreation of culture, 4–5, 53–57, 81
castes of in Caribbean, 65–67
conditions leading to migration, 17–25
cultural continuity, 10, 62–65, 116
cyclical migration of, 25
economic subsistence of, 19–20
emigration of to Caribbean (1838-1920), 6
factors discouraging emigration, 25–26
geographic origins of emigrants, 27–29
Kala Pani as obstacle to emigration, 25
labour migration of, 13–18, 22
marital status, 27
non-Hindu aboriginal tribes, 27–28
patterns of integration, 64–65
repatriation, 7, 73
role of Indian philosophy on social structures, 85–86
See also Indo-Caribbeans
economic development, colonial mode of, 15–16
Eliot, Charles, 39
emancipation, effect on labour supply, 13–14, 15–16
emigrant labourers. *See* indentured labour
emigration
abolition of, 9
and adaptive capacity of indentured labour, 5–6
civil wars and, 22–23
of East Indians to Caribbean (1838–1920), 6
factors discouraging, 25–26
female-male ratio of emigrants, 91, 150n12
and free trade, 24
imperialism and, 18, 140n15
India Emigration Proceedings (1874), 52
and Indian nationalist movement, 8–9, 24–25
internal factors in, 10

and natural disasters, 20–22
personal reasons for, 23
quota system for women, 91
recruitment pattern in, 27–28
recruitment practices, 16, 23–25
suspicion of, 24–25
of women, 91–95
Emmer, Peiter, 102, 103
Engels, Friedrich, 45
the Enlightenment, and European expansion, 38–39
Essay on the Inequality of the Human Races (de Gobineau), 38
Europe
growth of as dominant force, 37–39
industrialization of, 15–17
Self/Other justification, 38–39
Europeans, as indentured labour, 6, 14
evangelical colonialism, 70–71, 109
evolutionary model of change, 62–63

famine, effect of on emigration, 21, 114
Ferguson, W.F., 31
Foucault, Michel, 37, 48–49
free trade, and movement of labour, 24
Freud, Sigmund, 59, 60–61

Gandhi, M.K., 68, 120
gender relations, 10
British colonial policy towards, 89–90, 104
father-son relationship, 82
female-male ratio of emigrants, 91, 150n12
under indenture system, 11–12, 65
inter-familial relationships, 83–84
interracial marriages, 101–2
in joint family system, 77
social violence and, 95–102
Geoghegan, John, 21
Gobineau, J.A. de, 38
gossip, as symbolic resistance, 58–59
Gramsci, Antonio, 36–37
grant money as incentive, 8
Guadeloupe, Indo-Caribbean indenture in, 67

Guyana
  Indo-Caribbean indenture in, 3, 67
  Indo-Caribbeans as majority population, 7
Haraksingh, Kusha, 40
Heath, Roy, 59
hegemony, 36–37
Herbert, R.G.W., 33
hidden transcript of power relations, 11, 44, 46–49, 115
hierarchization, in colonial societies, 4, 42
"Hill Coolies", 27–28
Hinduism, 39
  and caste expulsion, 25
  caste system in, 29, 65–66
  cultural continuity and, 116, 146n61
  Dharma, 66
  Karma, 66
  Maya, 66
  respect for women in, 89
  role of Brahmans in indentured communities, 74–75
Hobsbawn, Eric, 49, 55
Hoggart, Richard, 48
honour killings, 95
hooks, bell, 100
humour, in power relationships, 59–61, 76
hybridity, 105–6
hybridization, 63
imperialism
  as civilizing mision, 14
  defined, 15
  and East Indian emigration, 18
  emergence of, 38–39
  and labour migration, 13, 140n15
  metropolitan-colonial relationship and, 15–17
  role of in labour recruitment, 33–34
  socioeconomic oppression under, 23
  and world capitalism, 10
indentured communities
  breakdown of caste system in, 72–76
  land ownership in, 81, 84

Panchayat system, 99
social stratification in, 74–75
village system in, 53–54
indentured labour
  adaptive capacity of, 109–10, 119–20
  age of, 27
  caste composition, 29
  death rate at sea, 28
  gender disparity in, 78, 91
  geographic origins, 27–29
  incentives to stay in Caribbean, 8, 80
  land ownership as incentive, 81, 84, 94, 111, 112
  linguistic codes of, 57–58
  linguistic diversity of, 30
  living conditions of, 72
  marital status, 27
  occupations of, 30
  political clout of, 35
  religious composition, 29–30
  return passage rights, 73, 80
  "shanghaiing" of, 32
  social ties of, 81
  wages, 7, 104, 111
indentured service
  abuse of labourers, 7
  desertion from, 50–51
  as labour contract system, 7
  overview, 6–9
  phases of, 6
  primary resistance to, 49–53
  symbolic resistance to, 49, 53–61
indenture system
  comparison to slavery, 6, 8, 31, 33, 40, 72, 79
  emancipation, 112, 117
  incentives to stay in Caribbean, 8, 80, 81, 84, 94, 111, 112
  Kamiuti, 19
  literature on, 3–6
  manipulation of by indentured labour, 10–11
  positive aspects of, 114, 118–19
  post-emancipation job structure, 42

primary resistance under, 49–53
regulations governing, 7–8, 80
research sources, 9–10
symbolic resistance under, 36, 49, 53–61
as victimization, 108
India
abolition of slavery in, 19
domestic problems as cause of emigration, 34
effect of British colonialism on labour migration, 16–18
effect of natural disasters on emigration, 20–22
"Hill Coolies", 27–28
impact of British colonialism on, 17–18
labour migration within, 13
land revenue system, 17–18
"Madras Coolies", 28–29
nationalist movement in, 8–9, 24–25
non-Hindu aboriginal tribes, 27–28
role of women in, 87–91
rural economy of, 26
social reform towards women, 89–90
village system in, 20
An Indian Slave Trade (Herbert), 33
Indo-Caribbeans
education, 112
financial achievements of, 111–12
as majority population, 3, 7, 68
recreation of culture, 4–5, 81, 116
role of Indian philosophy on social structures, 85–86
social mobility, 111, 112–14
transition to class system, 72–76
and Western laws, 68
See also East Indians
industrial residence, 7
Industrial Revolution, 15–17, 38–39
interactional model of change, 62–63
inter-capitalist competition, 15–17
internal colonialism, 4
interracial marriages, 101–2

Jahaji Bhai/Bahin, 81
Jaimini, Metha, 73

Jain, Ravindra, 102
Japan, use of humour to resist domination, 60
jati identity, 26, 69
Jayawardena, Chandra, 55, 56–57, 83–84
Jha, J.C., 21
joint family system, 76–86
in Caribbean society, 63, 64–65, 77–80, 81–82
compositional categories of, 76–77
as coping mechanism, 85
father-son relationship, 82
inter-familial relationships, 83–84
jati (extended family system), 26
and labour migration, 22
property inheritance, 76
social reform towards women, 90

Kala Pani as obstacle to emigration, 25
Kamiuti, 19
Kanhai, Rosanne, 106
kidnapping, as form of recruitment, 33
Klass, Morton, 64

labour displacement, 16
labour migration
and free trade, 24
in India, 13–17, 22, 113–14
push/pull model of, 10, 14–15
laissez-faire economics, 24
Lamming, George, 110
land incentives, 8, 80–81, 94, 111, 112
land revenue system, 17–18
language
development of linguistic codes, 57–58
as hindrance to emigration, 26
linguistic diversity, 30
Pidgin, 57
planters use of to create disunity, 57
Laurence, Keith, 34, 52, 67
Lautour, E.F., 18–19
Lenin, V.I., 23
Levine, Lawrence, 53
Lowenthal, David, 41

Macaulay, Thomas Babington, 14
"Madras Coolies", 28–29
Mahabir, Jules, 73
Malthus, Thomas, 21
Malthusian population theory, 21
marginalization, in colonial societies, 4
Maroons, 51
marriage customs
    child marriage, 90, 151n36
    interracial marriages, 101–2
    legalization of, 73
    maintenance of in Caribbean society, 64–65
    recognition of, 94–95
Martinique, Indo-Caribbean indenture in, 67
Marx, Karl, 45, 53, 77
Mati, 56
Matikor, 106–7
Mauritius, 31
McNeil-Lal Report, 96
mercantilism, 18
migration, of East Indians, conditions leading to, 17–25
migration theories
    effect of British colonialism on labour migration, 16–18
    international migration labour theory, 16–17
    push/pull model of, 10, 14–15, 23
Mintz, Sidney, 41
Mitchell, Robert, 25, 28–29, 93
Mittelholzer, Edgar, 111
Moore, Brian, 51, 103
Morris, H.S., 69
Morton, John, 71
Muharram Massacre (Trinidad), 50, 55–56
multiculturalism, 63
Murdoch, Clinton, 108

Naipaul, V.S., 4
natural disasters, effect of on emigration, 20–22
neutralization in delinquency, 99–100
Nevadomsky, Joseph, 64
A New System of Slavery (Tinker), 30

Niehoff, A. and J., 64–65
nigger yards, 72
non-Europeans, as indentured labour, 6, 7
nuclear family, 63
    and joint family system, 85

Omvedt, Gail, 25

Panchayat system, 99
Parson, Talcott, 63–64
pass system, 50–51, 52, 109
Patterson, Orlando, 48
People's Association of British Guiana, 73
Persaud, Sital, 73
Petras, Elizabeth, 35
Phillips, Leslie, 100
Pidgin, development of, 57
plantation system
    and caste system breakdown, 67–72
    effect of slave emancipation on, 6
    during emancipation period, 41–42
    emigrant preferences of planters, 29, 34, 35, 78, 92–93
    incentives of, 81
    and joint family system, 78–79
    labour conditions, 30, 109
    labour scarcity in, 10
    living conditions, 8
    manipulation of by indentured labour, 5–6, 10–11
    post-emancipation job structure of, 42
    power and domination of planter class, 39–41
    repression against primary resistance, 52
    role of in breakdown of societal norms, 99–100
    rural isolation policy of, 65
    sugar production and, 4, 8
Plural Society Theory, 63
Portes, Alejandro, 16
power relations
    hidden transcript of, 44, 46–49
    institutionalization of, 42

public transcript of, 44–49
Premdas, Ralph, 64
primary resistance, 49–53
public transcript of power relations, 44–49

racial hostility, towards Indo-Caribbeans, 74
Reactance Theory, 51
Reckless, Walter, 99
recruitment practices, 3, 4
   abuse of labourers, 31
   crimping, 23–24, 32
   deception in, 23–25, 28, 31
   displaced labourers, 17–18
   and East Indian cultural mores, 25–26
   "Madras Coolies", 28–29
   money advances, 34
   non-Hindu aboriginal tribes, 27–28
   regional preferences of agents, 27–29
   regulations governing, 8, 16, 32, 92
   "shanghaiing" of labourers, 32
   for women, 34–35
Reddock, Rhoda, 102, 104
relief theory, of laughter, 61
religion(s)
   and cultural continuity, 116, 146n61
   of emigrants, 29–30, 66
   evangelical colonialism, 70–71
   religious asceticism of women, 89
Renard, R., 67
Repak, Terry, 16
repatriation
   land settlements and, 94, 112
   return passage rights, 73, 80
   and unfavourable reports by returned emigrants, 25–26
resistance
   codes of, 55
   covert actions, 11
   and cultural adaptivity, 114–16
   desertion as, 50–51
   by indentured labour, 5, 10
   in indenture system, 10–11, 40
   mimic individuals and, 107

   overt actions, 11
   primary resistance, 49–53
   self-control and, 53
   solidarity and, 56
   subversive resistance, 46–49
   suicide as, 50
   symbolic resistance, 36, 49, 53–61, 115–16
return passage rights, 73, 80
rice industry, development of, 110
Robertson, I.C., 34
Rodney, Walter, 109
Rodway, James, 110
Roy, Rajaram Mohan, 90
Ruhoman, Joseph, 73
Ruhoman, Peter, 73
ryotwari land revenue system, 17–18

Said, Edward, 38–39, 103
Samaroo, Brinsley, 4
Sanatan Dharma (Eternal Religion), 71
Sanderson Commission, 32
Sanderson Committee, 22
Sandhu, Kernial, 19
sati, 88–89, 90, 104
Scott, James, 44, 46, 49, 55
Seecharan, Clem, 56
Senart, Emile, 65
Sepoy Mutiny, 22–23
sexual abuse, 10, 101, 109
sexual exploitation, 100–101, 151n36
The Shadow Bride (Heath), 59
sharecropping
   in India, 19, 20
   in United States, 47
Sharma, Labehari, 4
Sharpe, Jenny, 107
Shaw, Nate, 47
Shepherd, Verene, 3, 101
Singer, Milton, 76
Singh, Kelvin, 50, 55–56, 120
Singh, Lutchman, 73
Single Men in Barracks (Phillips), 100
slavery

abolition of in India, 19
comparison to indenture system, 6, 8, 31, 33, 40, 72, 79, 108
effect of emancipation on labour supply, 6, 10, 13–14, 15–16
Kamiuti, 19
Smith, Adam, 24
Smith, M.G., 63
Smith, Raymond, 29–30, 63–64, 67, 83–84
social customs, as hindrance to emigration, 26
Social Darwinism, 14
social violence, gender relations and, 95–102
South Africa, use of humour to resist domination, 60
Spain, request for indentured labour, 7
Spivak, Gayatri, 104
spousal abuse, 95–102
Stark, James, 110
Stembridge, E.C., 110
subordinate classes
  transcripts of power relations, 44–49
  Uncle Tom behaviour, 45
sugar industry
  increased production of, 110
  labour requirements, 4, 8, 12, 110
  metropolitan-colonial relationship and, 15
  pull factor of migration, 23
suicide, 50, 82–83, 109
Suriname
  Indo-Caribbean indenture in, 3
  Indo-Caribbeans as majority population, 7
  Suriname Immigrants' Association, 73
Swami Dayananda, 90
symbolic resistance, 49, 53–61, 115–16
  and development of linguistic codes, 57–58
  gossip as, 58–59
  humour as, 59–61

Tinker, Hugh, 4
  A New System of Slavery, 30
transportation, regulations governing, 8
Trinidad
  East Indian National Congress, 73
  Indo-Caribbean indenture in, 3, 67
  Indo-Caribbeans as majority population, 7
  sugar production in, 110
Trinidad Working Men's Association, 73

Uganda, caste system in, 68–69
Uncle Tom behaviour, 45
United States, use of humour to resist domination, 60

vagrancy laws, 52
Vidyasager, 90

Walcott, Derek, 53–54, 55, 146n61
Wales, W.S., 32
Wallerstein, Immanuel, 15
Weber, Max, 64
wife murders, 97–99, 109
Williams, Eric, 14, 109
Williams, Raymond, 103
Wolf, Eric, 20, 41
women
  categories of emigrants, 96
  double oppression of, 104
  female infanticide, 90
  female-male ratio of emigrants, 91, 150n12
  historical attitude of, 87–89
  "housewifization", 102
  and hybridity, 105–6, 117
  inheritance rights, 90
  in joint family system, 82–83, 86
  kidnapping of, 33
  legal position of in India, 90
  Matikor, 106–7
  medical examination of, 26, 92
  position of under indenture system, 11–12, 117
  recruitment of, 33, 34–35
  religious asceticism of, 89
  role of in India, 87–91
  sati, 88–89, 90, 104
  sexual abuse of, 10, 101
  sexual exploitation of, 100–101, 151n36
  shortage of as emigrants, 91–95
  spousal abuse, 95–102

suicide of, 82–83
the Third Space, 102–7, 117
wage differentials of, 104
wife murders, 97–99, 109
work stoppages as resistance, 50
world capitalism
    and disruption of social customs, 20
    effect on labour migration, 24
    emergence of, 38–39

labour costs, 16
patriarchal aspect of, 35
push/pull model of labour migration, 10, 14–15, 32
role of in indenture system, 10, 15
and rural decline, 18

zamindari land revenue system, 17–18